Instructor's Resource Kit
Gwen Spencer

Keys to Success
How to achieve your goals

Carol Carter · Sarah Lyman Kravits

Prentice Hall
Upper Saddle River, NJ 07458

©1996 Prentice-Hall, Inc.
A Simon & Schuster Company
Upper Saddle River, NJ 07458

10   9   8   7   6   5   4   3   2   1

ISBN 0-13-233172-1

Printed in the United States of America

Table of Contents

Dear Fellow Educator,

Today colleges and universities face the challenge of educating an increasingly diverse and complex student body. Enrollment trends indicate that the growing constituencies include ethnic minority students, commuters, older adult learners and students with disabilities. All of these student populations place new demands upon institutions of higher learning that are already facing shrinking resources and greater accountability. Student diversity is not the only challenge confronting colleges and universities. Students, in general, are more skeptical of authority, less accustomed to doing homework, and more aware of their role as a consumer. Clearly university educators have many significant issues to consider in creating a meaningful, hospitable classroom experience for students.

At the same time that institutions of higher learning are experiencing educational challenges, there is a growing national need for a skilled and flexible work force. Perhaps, more than at any previous time in history, the future of our society depends on the education of our citizens and the energy of our work force. Students graduating within the next three to five years will face a world that requires skills to think with wisdom and to act with vision.

Keys to Success is designed to bridge the gap between institutions of higher learning, the world of work, and the emerging student population. Authors Carter and Kravits recognize that students need more than study skills to succeed in this rapidly changing world. Students need learning strategies and life skills that give them a solid foundation for the future. While career competencies and life-long learning are important, it is equally important that students are able to identify their values and live out their commitments. Without this foundation, students may be unable to negotiate their future with clarity and confidence.

This resource manual offers educational classroom activities as well individual assignments that are designed to augment the content of the textbook. In addition, the manual's exercises are structured to encourage the development of critical thinking and communication skills. Furthermore, the class exercises facilitate cooperative learning and appreciation for diversity. Transparencies as well as suggestions for supplemental readings and media are offered for your use. And finally, suggested exam questions and other assessments are included at the end of every chapter. The final section of the manual features a number of "Best Teaching Strategies" that I hope are helpful to you.

As an instructor, your task is one that requires compassion and courage. According to Stephen Brookfield, professor of Higher and Adult Education at Columbia University, "Teaching is the educational equivalent of white-water rafting" (Brookfield, 1992. p.2). I hope that this educational resource manual assists you in negotiating the challenging rapids ahead.

Designing the Course, Defining the Expectations

Course Title Suggestions: Success Skills for College. Improvement in Learning Skills, College Learning Skills, University 101, Strategies for Learning and Living, Effective Learning Strategies, Becoming a Strategic Learner, Learning Skills for the Twenty-first Century, Keys for Success.

General Course Description: The purpose of this class is to provide students with the self awareness, learning strategies, academic skills and individual direction to succeed within the higher education environment as well as in the world of work. This class is structured to offer students practical, proactive approaches to manage the academic expectations and personal adjustment of college. Content for the course is drawn from a variety of disciplines including cognitive psychology, social psychology, wellness, and sociology. However, the emphasis is placed upon the application of these principles. Students are expected to be active partners in the learning environment of the class.

Target Student Audience for this Class: There is a wide variety of students who could benefit from the information offered in this course depending upon the needs and goals of your university. Particular students who might be targeted for this class include any or all of the following:

*New Freshman students.

*First year Transfer students attending your university.

*Students who are "underprepared" for college coursework.

*Students who are on academic probation.

*First generation college students who do not have family members to explain the university's ethos and expectations.

*College athletes who are juggling travel schedules, practices, and games along with their studies.

*International students who may not understand the American system of higher education.

Should various populations be integrated into the same class section?

In general, yes. The stimulation of working with different types of students and learning how others address educational and personal challenges can be an enriching experience.

However, various student sub-groups could benefit from experiencing this class as a homogeneous cohort. The cohort approach to the class can facilitate the formation of a support group network for students with more specialized needs or concerns that is English as a Second Language, college athletes, student parents, etc..

If you select to establish heterogeneous class sections, there may be times during the term when it may be useful to assign more homogeneous sub-groups of students to discussion groups so more individualized problem solving and support can occur.

Learning Objectives for the Student:

1. To develop greater insight into the student's current academic abilities and motivation in order to determine strengths and areas that may need development.

2. To explore strategies for enhancing personal motivation, competence, and discipline.

3. To define short-term as well as long-term goals within the professional, personal and educational spheres.

4. To introduce students to the campus resources and the ways they can efficiently access those resources.

5. To understand basic time management approaches that can be useful in creating productive study and work habits.

6. To learn and practice active listening.

7. To define the value and venues for establishing meaningful relationships with university faculty and staff.

8. To learn about the concepts of learning style and how to use learning style to maximize their learning efforts.

9. To enhance reading and notetaking strategies that aid learning and critical analysis.

10. To develop skills for approaching objective and essay exams.

11. To acquire problem solving skills by using analysis and critical thinking.

12. To refine writing skills for clear and concise communication.

13. To become familiar with issues of wellness that enhance peak performance academically and personally.

14. To explore the value of a college education and some of the trends occurring on college campuses.

15. To identify the competencies and attitudes that employers are looking for in their employees.

16. To gain an understanding of the transitions college student experience and ways to deal with the stresses inherent in the changes and adjustments.

17. To learn how to use financial and resource management skills for use as a student and as a professional.

18. To deepen understanding of students' abilities, interests and values.

19. To develop enhanced skills in critical thinking and creative problem solving.

20. To work together in a respectful an open fashion.

Suggested Grading Policy:

Depending upon whether your university subscribes to a quarter or semester system, you may adjust the number of assignments for the students.

Because this course is intended to assist students in their skill building and self awareness, the focus for the student evaluation is portfolio assignments and personal reflection papers and/or journal entries.

The elimination of a grading curve may encourage more cooperative learning and application of the concepts. It is suggested that you consider using a point system that encourages individual initiative and not competition among the students. A suggested point system is explained in the following.

Grading Policy Considerations:

1. Grades are based on the total number of points that the student earns in the class.

2. Every assignment has a designated point value. Assignments receive full or partial point value depending on the quality, thoroughness, and punctuality of the work. Assignments submitted after the due date will be considered late by the instructor unless there are unusual circumstances that will need to be explained to the instructor. Point deletions for lateness will be determined at the instructor's discretion.

3. Class attendance is mandatory and will be considered in determining the grade of an individual student. Every class missed without a reasonable excuse will result in the loss of points toward the final grade. As the instructor, you may decide to allow for a designated number of unexcused absences and then any absence beyond the "free misses" could result in some penalty, but it is better to avoid this option.

4. Performance expectations could include any of the following:

> *A designated number of portfolio assignments including some or all of the Individual Assignments at the end of each chapter. Or you might request one sample activity from each of the chapters or the manual being submitted. This approach would allow students to select the activity that seems more meaningful and relevant to their needs and interests.

> *One to three tests or exams.

> *Student Journaling Activities.

*One to three personal reflection papers.

*Participation in the Classroom Activities.

*Attendance and class involvement.

*Attendance at a campus event like a play, recital, or a forum.

5. Point values for assignments are determined by the instructor.

6. Total points will be tabulated and evaluated using the following scale:

100-94% = A
93-92% = A-
91-89% = B+
88-84% = B
83-82% = B-
81-79% = C+
78-74% = C
73-72% = C-
71-69% = D+
68-64% = D
63-62% = D-
61% and below is failing.

Writing Assignment Expectations:

All papers submitted by students should be typed and double spaced. Students should have a one-inch margin around the text and use a twelve font type size. Papers are graded using the following criteria: content, organization, clarity, and grammatical structure such as tense agreement, punctuation, and spelling. Generally, a point distribution system for the grading of papers is appreciated by the students so they have a better idea of what areas in their writing need improvement. For example, the content could be worth 50% of the grade, the organization and clarity could be worth 25% of the grade, and the grammatical structure could be worth 25% of the grade.

For users of the

KEYS TO SUCCESS/
NCS *Career Assessment Inventory*
Package

To the Instructor

Congratulations! You chose the best in career counseling products when you selected the Career Assessment Inventory - The Enhanced Version from NCS! We've combined an effective and versatile career interest inventory with the efficiency of computerized data entry, scoring, and reporting.

The Purpose of this Guide:

- Discuss the functionality and benefits of interest inventories and career assessments

- Help you facilitate group interpretations using the Career Assessment Inventory

By taking advantage of the ability to perform group interpretations with the Career Assessment Inventory, you efficiently guide students through an exciting and potentially life changing encounter with an analysis of their interest patterns and how they compare with over 100 contemporary occupations.

This guide is not intended to explain the construction and psychometrics of the test. For this level of information, we recommend that you refer to the Career Assessment Inventory Manual.

Included with this guide you will find several helpful masters that you can reproduce and use in your interpretation sessions. Also included for your convenience:

- a sample Student Action Planning Guide
- a Student's Guide to help explain their test results, and

Each of these practical counseling aids can be used "as is" or customized to best meet your unique needs.

We are pleased to provide you with this guide to group interpretations of the Career Assessment Inventory. If you have any comments or suggestions about this guide, please forward them to:

Kevin Anderson
Product Manager
National Computer Systems
P.O. Box 1416
Minneapolis, MN 55440
Fax: 612-939-5099

Background Information

Purpose of an interest inventory:

- Focus attention (too many choices can be confusing, or lack of awareness on interests can feel limiting)
- Guide discussion
- Facilitate action planning
- Create realistic hopes and dreams

Three Type of Career Decision-Making

"The Flounderer"

- This entails going from job to job to job or major to major to major
- No aim or focus
- No motivation, commitment or passion
- Might stumble onto something that fits the person

"Divine Insight"

- This entails waiting for a "sign" or a special feeling about what direction, job, or major to pursue prior to taking actio
- Out of a fear of making the wrong choice, no choice is made at all

"Target Occupational Range"

- This entails a systematic process of exploring several occupations
- Utilizing an interest inventory to provide an initial starting point for career exploration, the individual creates a plan
- The individual believes that several types of work could be win/win situations
- Networks with friends, family, and professionals to learn about the industry/occupation/open positions
- Arranges informational interviews
- Persistent and consistent efforts result in the confidence necessary to get that "first job"

Prior to the Group Interpretation Session

- Identify 6 areas of your room in which students can stand to identify with their highest General Theme Score
  - Ideas: Create 8.5" x 11" - sized letters of R, A, I, S, E, & C and tape in the designated area of the room
- Create a continuum of scores ("less than 42", "43-56", & "greater than 57" is probably adequate) to represent the potential scale scores on the inventory
  - Ideas: tape numbers written on 8.5" x 11" sheets of paper around the room, write numbers on the chalk/white board, or verbally describe the low end and the high end to the class
- Determine which four Basic Interest Areas to use in the group exercise (choose two similar and two dissimilar)

Group Interpretation Session Outline

Brief overview of Career Assessment Inventory
- Refer to it as an "inventory" rather than a "test — less threatening
- Measures interests, not aptitude or ability
- Describe the purpose of an interest inventory (see above)
- Inventory results provide information concerning how interest preferences relate to the world of work
    - Group interpretation session helps students gain a perspective on how similar or unique one's interests are compared to peers
    - Many options available in the world of work and virtually all careers are available to everyone regardless of their gender
    - Encourage participants to think openly about all possibilities and not reflect on stereotypes

Explain organization of the profile reports

- Broad to narrow orientation in presentation
    - Broad: General Themes Scales
    - Less broad: Basic Interest Area Scales
    - Specific: Occupational Scales
- Notice the color themes
    - The color associated with the General Theme scale is applied to the corresponding Basic Interest Area Scales and Occupational Scales

General Themes Scales (Overhead)

- Measures broad orientation to the world of work
    - Major categories or descriptors of types work
- Stress that all descriptors for the scale may not fit each individual
- Most people don't fit neatly into just one scale but share characteristics of many
- High scores are obtained by a general liking for the activities in those areas

Characteristics of Realistic - "Doers" (Overhead)
- Robust, Rugged, Physically Strong
- Uncomfortable in Social Settings
- Good Motor Coordination
- Mechanically, Athletically Oriented
- Conservative Political Views
- Don't Participate in the Arts and Sciences
- Like to Build with Tools, Work with Hands
- Like to Work Outdoors
- Cool to Radical New Ideas
- Like to Work with Big, Powerful Machines
- Buy Boats, Campers, Snowmobiles, Motorcycles, Tools, Sports Equipment
- View Life as Straightforward Rather Than Complex

Characteristics of Investigative - "Thinkers" (Overhead)
- Science Oriented, Understand Laws of Nature
- All Wrapped Up in Their Work, Problem Oriented
- Inner Oriented, Unsociable
- Strong Need to Understand the World, Test Out Ideas
- Enjoy Tasks Where Process and Answers are Unclear
- Prefer to Work Alone
- Feel Lacking in Leadership Skills
- Confident of Intellectual Abilities
- Curious, Reserved, Independent, Analytical
- Buy Telescopes, Calculators, Electronic Equipment
- View Life as something to Discover

Characteristics of Artistic - "Creators" (Overhead)
- Art, Music, Creative Interests
- Avoid Working with Rules, Structure
- Value Beauty in All Forms
- Rely on Intuition vs. Logic
- Like Small, Intimate Groups
- Willing to Take Risks
- Dress in Freer Styles than Other People
- Not Assertive About Own Capabilities
- Sensitive and Emotional
- Frequent Art Galleries, Concerts, Plays, Art Fairs
- Buy Art Objects, Books, Paintings
- View Life as Opportunity to Express Themselves

Characteristics of Social - "Helpers" (Overhead)
- Sociable, Responsible, Humanistic, Religious
- Like Working in Groups
- Speaking and People Skills
- Enjoy Helping, Enlightening, Training, Curing, Teaching, Guiding Others
- Avoid Physical Exertion
- Understanding, Idealistic
- Dislike Working with Machines, Structure
- Like Philosophical Questions
- Cooperative, Friendly, Generous, Caring
- Attend Lots of Workshops, Other Group Experiences
- View Life as Opportunity to Serve Others

Characteristics of Enterprising - "Persuaders" (Overhead)
- Speaking Skills, Persuasive
- Strong Leaders
- Dislike Science, Systematic Thinking
- Strong Drive to Attain Personal, Work Goals
- Like Power, Status, Leadership
- Popular, Self-Confident, Sociable, Assertive
- High Energy Level, Make Things Happen
- Adventuresome, Ambitious
- Value Money, Material Possessions
- Buy Big Cars, Nice Cloths, Country Club Memberships
- View Life in Terms of Power, Status, and Material Wealth

Characteristics of Conventional - "Organizers" (Overhead)
- Like Organized Environments, What's Expected
- Avoid People Problems
- Conscientious, Efficient, Practical, Orderly
- Like to Associate with Power
- Value Material Possessions, Status
- Orderly, Persistent, Calm
- Don't Like to Lead
- Stable, Well-Controlled, Dependable
- Save Money, Buy Conservative Things - Furniture, House
- View Life as Predictable and Orderly - a Place for Everything and Everything in Its Place

Basic Interest Area Scales
- Measures individual's preferences for a focused scope of related activities
- Subscales of the corresponding General Themes Scales
- High scores are obtained by a general liking for the activities in those areas

Occupational Scales
- Indicates how one's likes and dislikes compare with employed people in that occupation
- Scores of 45 and higher indicate considerable interest similarity with people in the occupation
    - Occupations related to high scores should be highlighted as potential career possibilities and coordinated with information from other areas of the Career Assessment Inventory report, and other information about the individual, such as aptitude, skills, values, personality, and past experiences.
- Scores between 26 and 44 are in the range obtained by most people NOT in the occupation
    - Color-coded profile uses open bar to indicate females and shaded bar to indicate males NOT in the occupation
- Scores of 25 and lower indicate considerable interest dissimilarity with people in the occupation
    - The tasks and day-to-day functions of the occupation are areas of disinterest by the individual
    - Insight can be gained by identifying what you don't like about those occupations or tasks

Group Exercise

"Gather around the letter that matches your highest score" (e.g. if your highest score on the six General Themes is A, then stand by the Letter A in the room)

- Starting with R, stand by the subgroup and ask them about their hobbies (Overhead)
- Read scale characteristics and ask group if it sounds like them

(Repeat the process for the remaining five scales)

Basic Interest Area Scales

- Choose a Basic Interest Area scale and have the participants rank order themselves to reflect their score on the chosen scale; have them cluster in three groups: 42 and lower, 43-57, and 57+.
    - Allow participants to option of standing in the middle if one's score is embarrassing or would make them feel uneasy
        - e.g., One scores low on the Protective Services scale and is at a military school, or scores low on the Religious Activities scale and is at a religious institution
    - At each location, participants further sort themselves from high to low
    - Encourage interactions and notice those near them and those at a distance
- High scores are obtained by a general liking for the activities in those areas
- Discuss with participants scoring towards the high end their hobbies, leisure activities and likes
- Do the same with participants on the low end
- Continue process with a second chosen scale that concerns different interests than the first one, but is related to the general work domain
    - Relatively little movement should occur
- Choose third scale that illustrates opposite interests to those of the previous two scales. Have participants rearrange their order based on their scores on the third scale
    - Considerably more movement should occur from high to low and vice versa
- Continue process with a fourth scale that emphasizes positively related interests to the third scale
- Briefly discuss additional scales of interest to participants
- Have participants take their seats

Administrative Indices & Non-occupational Scales (Overheads)

- Details how the student responded to the test and provides additional information related to career exploration
- Total Responses, Response Patterning
- Fine Arts—Mechanical, Occupational Extroversion-Introversion, Educational Orientation, Variability of Interests

Reiterate that many options are available in the world of work and virtually all careers are available to everyone regardless of their gender

Encourage participants to think openly about all possibilities and not to reflect on stereotypes—also to develop a plan of action

Student Action Planning Guide

Name: _____   Date: _____

Step One: Determine Your Overall Interest Code

Find the General Themes section on your Career Assessment Inventory report and circle your three highest scores. Notice that each scale is identified by an initial, either R, I, A, S, E, or C. These initials will be used to determine your code. Select the letter of your highest score and write the letter in the box below next to the General Themes. Do the same for the second and third highest scores.

Find the Basic Interest Area Scales on your report and circle your three or four highest scores. The capital letter to the left of each group corresponds to the General Theme associated with that particular interest area. For example, if your highest interests are in sales, medical service, and educating, the corresponding themes would be Social (S) and Enterprising (E). To arrive at a letter code, rank the themes by considering both your highest scores as well as the balance among scores. Write your two- or three-letter code reflecting the themes for your strongest Basic Interest Areas.

Locate the Occupational Scales on your report. Circle the asterisks that are in the similar and very similar columns. Now circle those occupational titles with high scores that you would like to investigate. Each Occupational Scale is grouped according to its primary theme (the first letter of the code next to the occupational title). Indicate the two- or three-letter code which corresponds to the majority of your interests. Write this code in the box below.

Use the information in the box below to determine your Overall Interest Code. Write down the letter that appears most often. This is the first letter of your code. The second and third letters of the code will be the second and third most common letters among the boxes.

General Themes Code:	
Basic Interest Area Code:	
Occupational Scales Code:	
Overall Interest Code:	

Compare the letters in the Overall Interest Code to your personal preferences. Make any adjustments in the Overall Interest Code based on your knowledge of the themes and your vocational preferences. This code represents your strongest interests.

Step Two: Explore Occupations of Interest

Now it's time to explore the occupations that interest you. Use the occupations that you circled on your Career Assessment Inventory report as a starting point, but don't limit your exploration to these occupations. Use your Overall Interest Code to broaden your search. Several publications, such as the Occupational Outlook Handbook and the Dictionary of Occupational Titles, will provide information on specific occupations. Additionally, some computer databases organize occupational information according to the Holland theory codes you derived. Check with your instructor to find out which resources are available locally.

When learning about specific occupations, ask yourself the following questions:

> What is the nature of the work?
> What are the educational requirements for this occupation?
> What skills are needed for the occupation?
> What is the employment outlook?
> What are the working conditions?
> What do I like about this occupation?
> What don't like about this occupation?

Set up informational interviews to learn more about the day-to-day activities involved in specific occupations.

Take classes or do volunteer work in fields that interest you. Keep refining your occupational options as you get more information.

Determine an occupational field you want to pursue and work towards it. Keep in mind that on the average, an individual makes 5-6 major career changes in their lifetime. The occupational choice you make now can, and probably will change, as you learn more about yourself and the world of work.

Understanding the Career Assessment Inventory - A Student's Guide

The scores shown on the report form are from your responses provided to the Career Assessment Inventory. These scores are based on like and dislike answers to the inventory, and can be important in helping you better understand how your interests fit into the world of work.

The scores can provide helpful information or may tell you little more than you already know; however, they will help determine how high or low your interests are in a given area in comparison to the interests of others. The scores will also reveal interest areas previously unconsidered.

Most importantly, remember that the scores are measures of interests and not abilities. Factors such as ability, past life experiences, personality, and educational training are other important considerations. For example, a set of scores may show that the student likes art or sales, but they will not reflect a talent or training for art or sales work.

Four main sets of scores are given on the report form: General Themes, which gives an overall view of general interests, as compared to those of adults in a general population; Basic Interest Area Scales, which tells about strength of your interests in specific areas, such as sales, writing, and carpentry, in comparison to those of adults in a general population; Occupational Scales, which tells how similar or dissimilar your interests are to those of others in various occupations, such as accountants, computer programmers, or librarians; and Administrative Indices, which give some overall indications on how you responded to the Inventory, measured on a "Like-Indifferent-Dislike" basis.

The Career Assessment Inventory groups interests into six very broad categories, each of which is described by a General Theme. Scores on each of these six Theme scales tell how high or low your interest is in comparison to people in the general population.

General Theme Scales

Realistic:	People with high Realistic scores like to work with their hands and tools, and like to build and fix things. They are considered Doers.
Investigative:	These people like activities and occupations that are related to science and mathematics. They enjoy working with ideas and words to find their own answers and solutions. They are considered Thinkers.
Artistic:	Those in this category like to create artistic things that mean something to them personally. They frequently describe themselves as imaginative, original and expressive. They are referred to as Creators.
Social:	People who have high scores on this scale tend to have a very strong concern for other people and like to help them solve personal problems. They are best described as Helpers.
Enterprising:	High scores in this category are people who are good at talking and using words to persuade other people. Often they are in sales work, and are clever at thinking of new ways to do things that lead and convince people. They are often thought of as Persuaders.
Conventional:	These people prefer activities and jobs where they know exactly what is expected of them and what they are supposed to do. Such people describe themselves as stable, moderate and dependable. They are often referred to as Organizers.

Basic Interest Area Scales
More specific than the General Themes, these scales break down each of the themes into more specific interest areas. These scales show the strength of your interest in a variety of pure types of areas, such Electronics, Mathematics & Sales. The higher the score in an area, the more you tend to like activities in that area.

Occupational Scales

While the Basic Interest Area Scales can indicate strong interest in a pure content area, the Occupational Scales provide finer measures of the preferences associated with a range of occupational groups. These scales indicate the degree of similarity of your interests to those of people who have been satisfactorily employed in an occupation for a number of years. In front of each Occupational Scale name are one, two or three capital letters that show how the scale relates to the General Themes. For example, the capital I and R in front of the Electronic Technician scale show that both I-Investigative interests and R-Realistic interests are related to this scale. The scale is coded IR and not RI, because it is related more closely to the I-Investigative Theme than to the R-Realistic Theme. Some of the occupational scales have only one letter in front of them. This indicates that that theme is the most important part of the scale and that none of the other theme interests play a significant role. You have the best chance of finding satisfaction if you select an occupation or related area for which your score is high. You have the least chance of satisfaction if you choose an occupation for which your score is low. If your answers to the inventory are different from those of people employed in a particular occupation, your score on the related Occupational scale is low, and you probably would not like the everyday routine of that occupation. If your answers to the inventory are similar to those of people employed in a particular occupation, your score on the related Occupational scale is high, and you probably would find the work rewarding. You are also strongly encouraged to consider an occupation or related career for which your score is considerably higher than average for your gender, even if your score is not in the similar to very similar range.

Administrative Indices & Non-Occupational Scales

Administrative Indices include response percentages for each of the three sections, as well as Total Number of Responses. The administrative indices section also includes scores on 4 non-occupational scales: Fine Arts; Mechanical Occupational Extroversion-Introversion; Educational Orientation and Variability of Interests. These scales reflect the individual's preferences toward type of work, work setting, and range of interests.

Your like and dislike responses have been scored on a broad range of general interests and specific occupational scales. You should not be totally set on any one particular occupation for which your score is high, especially at an early age. Remember, each person is unique, and no test can predict with perfect accuracy the many differences among individuals. The information on the report, together with other relevant information--skills, accomplishments, experiences, other test scores, and so forth--should be considered in making any career decision. These results should be used as guidelines in helping you to better understand your interests and career possibilities.

REPRODUCIBLE MASTERS

The following pages contain "masters" of counselor tools that will enhance your group interpretation session. These pages can be repoduced for educational and training purposes only.

General Theme Scales

REALISTIC

INVESTIGATIVE

ARTISTIC

SOCIAL

ENTERPRISING

CONVENTIONAL

Realistic – "Doers"

- Like to repair, build, & maintain things

- Like to see tangible results

- Mechanically, athletically oriented

- Described as doers, rugged, tough, practical

- Buy boats, campers, tools, motorcycles, sports equipment

Investigative - "Thinkers"

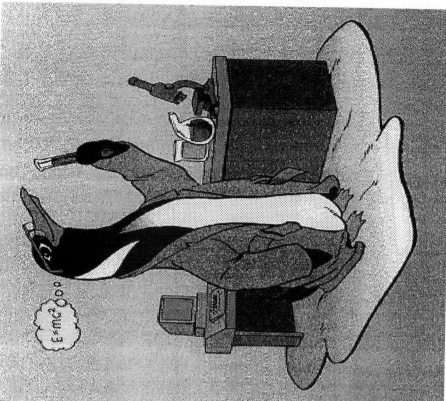

- Science or math oriented
- Prefer working alone
- Like to solve problems
- Described as thinkers, logical, rational, systematic, scientific
- Buy telescopes, calculators, electronic equipment

Artistic – "Creators"

- Like to work in creative endeavors

- Express themselves clearly

- Like unstructured environments - few rules

- Described as creators, musical, dramatic, introspective

- Buy art, books, paintings

Social – "Helpers"

- ◆ Enjoy helping, training and guiding others
- ◆ Prefer working with people
- ◆ Understand the feelings of others
- ◆ Described as helpers, humanistic, involved, sociable, talkative
- ◆ Attend workshops

Enterprising – "Persuaders"

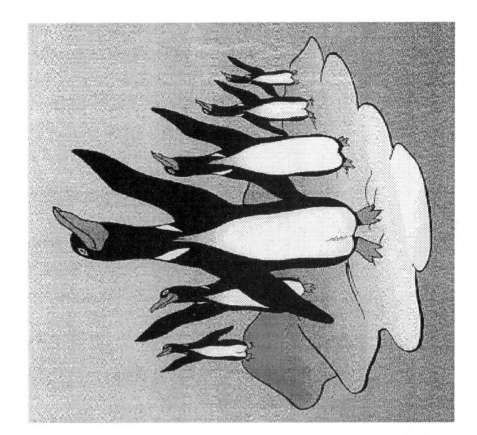

- ◆ Like power, status, and leadership
- ◆ Strong drive to attain goals
- ◆ Persuasive, confident
- ◆ Described as assertive, persuaders, ambitious, competitive
- ◆ Buy big cars, nice clothes, memberships

Conventional - "Organizers"

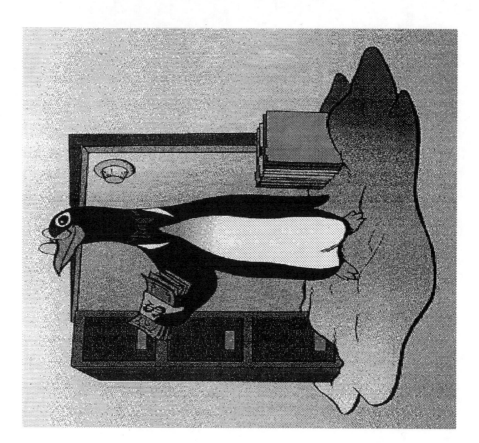

- Prefer structured environments
- Conscientious, efficient, practical
- Detail oriented
- Described as organizers, dependable, practical
- Save money, buy conservative things - furniture, houses

Administrative Indices:
Total Responses

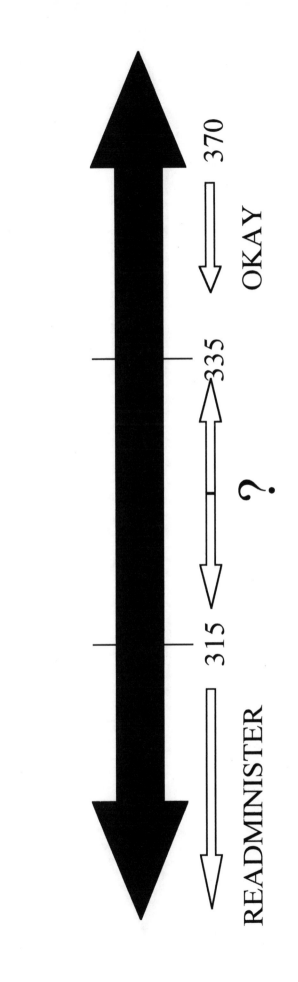

370

OKAY

335

?

315

READMINISTER

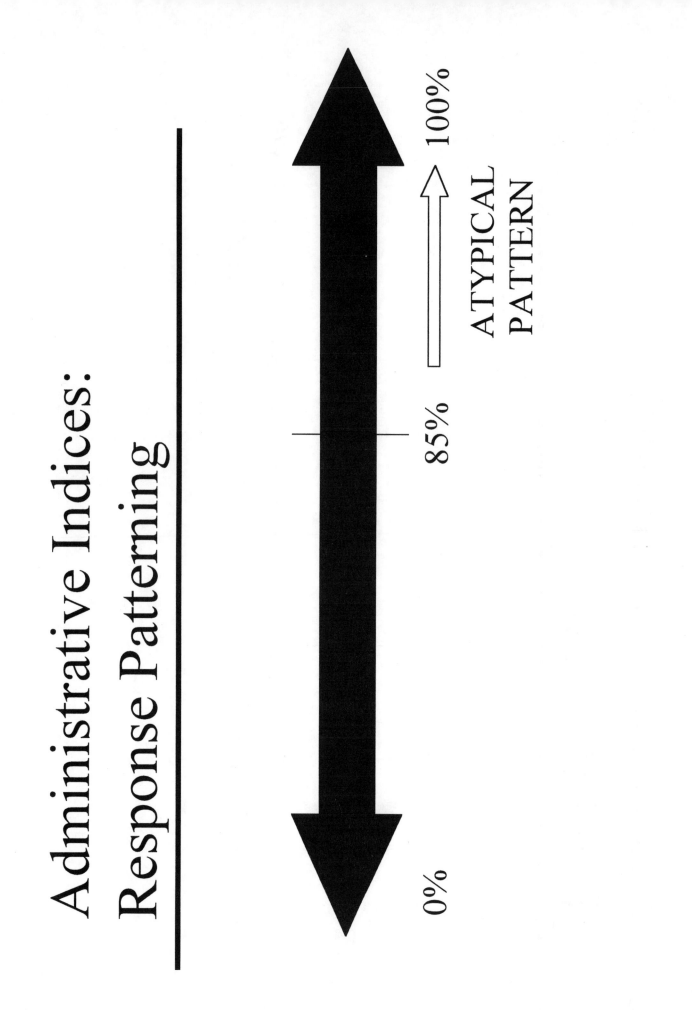

Administrative Indices:
Response Patterning

100%

ATYPICAL
PATTERN

85%

0%

Fine Arts - Mechanical

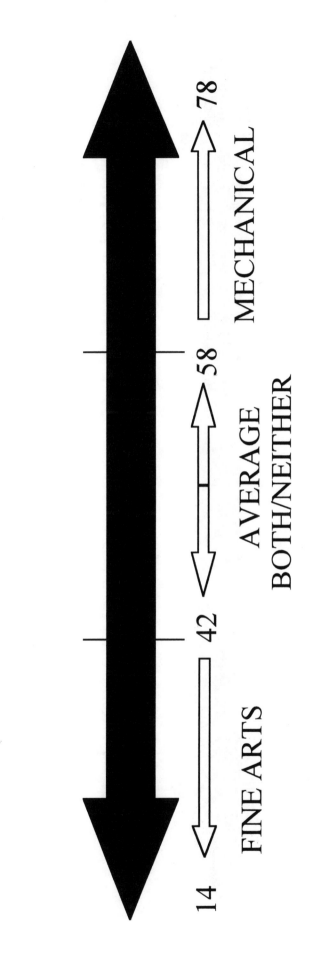

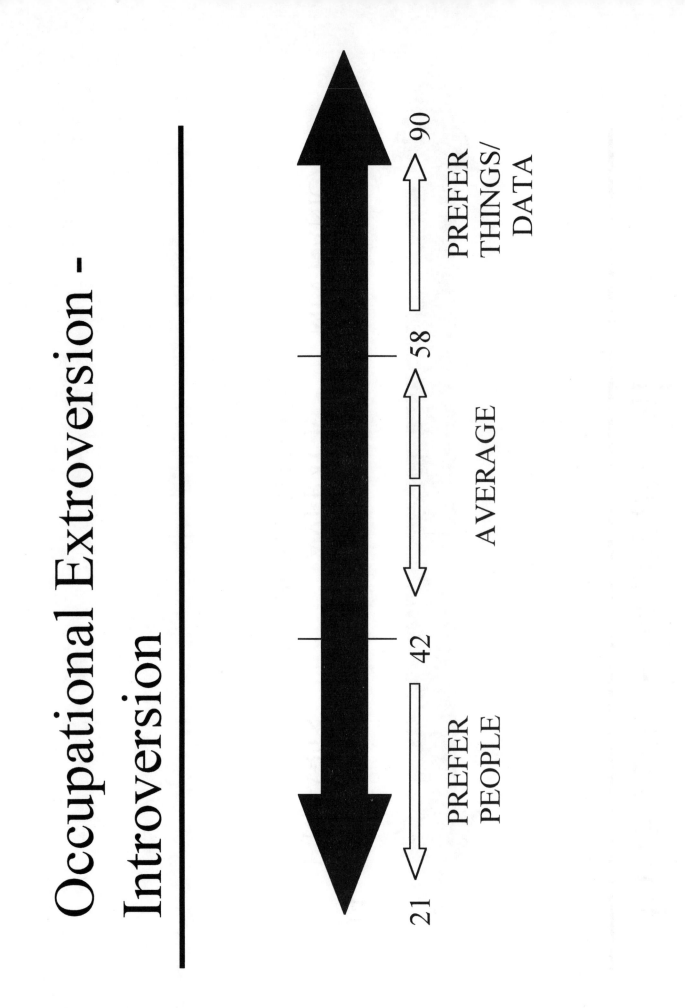

Educational Orientation

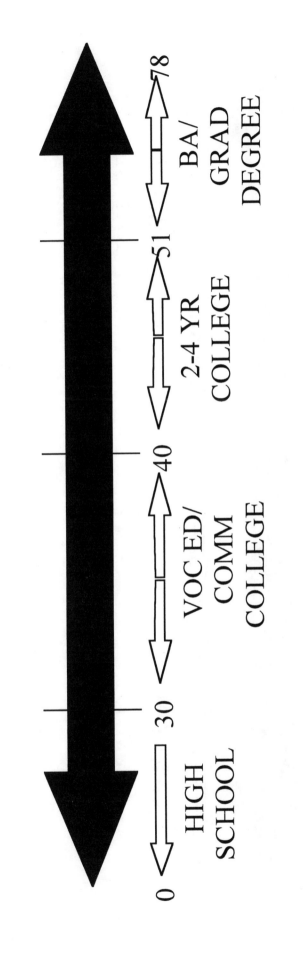

0   30   40   51   78

HIGH
SCHOOL

VOC ED/
COMM
COLLEGE

2-4 YR
COLLEGE

BA/
GRAD
DEGREE

Variability of Interests

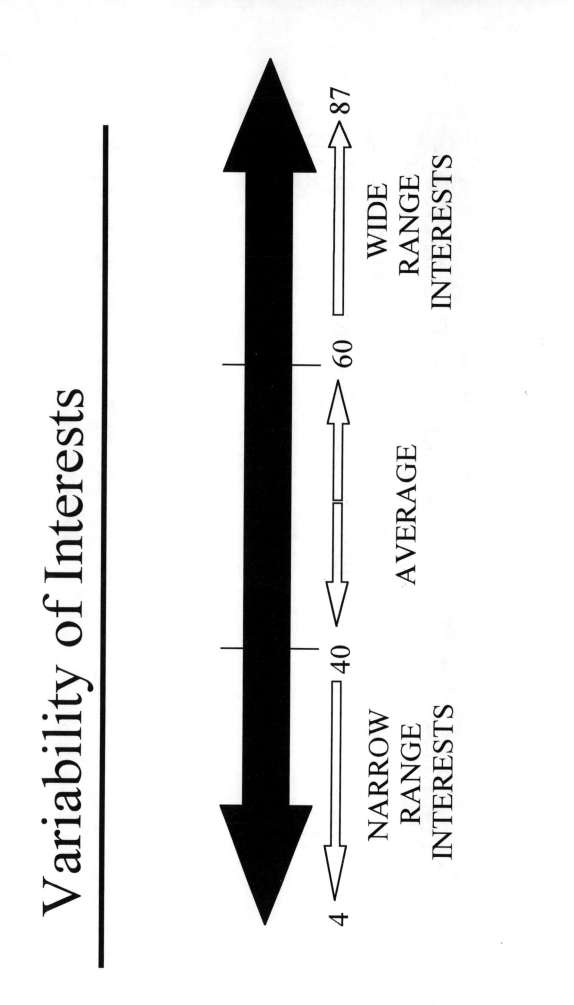

You are "Here", Aiming for "There"
Chapter 1

Key Concepts: This chapter highlights the changing student populations and their motivations for attending college. Students are encouraged to identify their own motives for attending school. Attitudes needed for success in college are presented, as well as a list of campus resources that are available to students while attending an institution of higher learning.

Additional Ideas to Explore with Students: A brief history of the American university can be helpful to many students in gaining some sense of the traditions and trends within higher education. Early in U.S. history, universities served primarily male, economically privileged, Caucasian students. Faculty and students lived and learned together on the campus and the university community was very homogeneous in terms of background and values. Today the Caucasian male student is actually a minority with almost 55% of the undergraduate student population composed of women. Ethnic minority students make up 20% of the undergraduate student population. International students represent approximately 4% of the total graduate and undergraduate population. The changing face of universities may be addressed in terms of your own local campus. A brief history of your university may be offered as part of an introduction to higher education.

Assisting students to clarify their own motivation for attending college is an important issue for students so they can sustain their focus and motivation for the next two or more years. One way to promote discussion of the students' educational motivation is to highlight the changes in student attitudes over the last quarter century. Alexander Astin's research with entering freshman students can be a stimulating way to engage students in exploring their values and educational expectations.

Individual Assignments

Each chapter in the instructor's manual features at least three suggested Individual Assignments for you to use or adapt as you deem appropriate. You may wish to assign other activities depending on the needs and interests of your class. The learning objective for each assignment and the teaching instructions are followed by handouts or other materials for you to duplicate.

Option I - Campus Resources

New students are frequently unaware of the valuable resources that are available to them on the campus. Many students are commuters and a significant percentage of the students are "first generation" college students. This activity introduces the students to many helpful resources as well as information about the campus.

The Campus Resources activity is similar to a scavenger hunt. The activity could be done individually or in small groups. Some orientation programs have provided each of the participating departments with one ingredient of "Trail Mix." When the students come to the office, they receive some peanuts, dried fruit, carob drops or some other ingredient. Bags can be distributed at the first stop.

Campus Resources

1. Hours of the Main Campus Library
   Monday-Thursday_____
   Friday_____
   Saturday_____
   Sunday_____

2. Where is the Counseling Center located? What are the hours for the Center? Are there any fees charged for the counseling services?
   _____
   _____
   _____

3. What overall Grade Point Average is needed to stay off of academic probation?_____

4. What is the minimum Grade Point Average that is required in the major that you are currently considering? Are there any classes that a student must complete prior to admission into the major?
   _____
   _____
   _____

5. To request a "Security Escort" on campus, what phone number do you need to use.
   _____

6. Name five good locations around the campus that would be conducive to your studying.
   _____
   _____
   _____
   _____

7. Does the campus offer tutoring services? Where could a student locate a tutor? Are there charges for tutoring support services?
   _____
   _____
   _____
   _____

8. Does the campus offer Career Development and Placement services? If yes, where is the office located? Who is the director of the Career Center? What specific services are offered?

_____

_____

_____

_____

_____

_____

9. When is the last day a student can enroll for a class during the current academic term?

_____

10. Is there an Exercise/ Weight Room for student use on the campus? If yes, where is it located?

_____

11. How does a student receive academic advising on this campus?

_____

_____

_____

_____

12. If a student wants to find out about getting involved with a club or an organization, where should he or she go to get information?

_____

_____

_____

Does this campus have an Amnesty International Chapter?_____

Is there an Accounting Club on campus?_____

Are there any campus clubs that you might want to join? _____

If yes, which one?_____

Option II - Three Peak Experiences

Students often are not aware of their own unique talents and experiences. Since many students must begin to determine what their major will be as well as a career direction, it is important for students to begin the process of becoming more self-aware and confident about their strengths and aspirations.

In this activity students look back over their personal history in order to recall what their accomplishments and significant experiences have been. Students must reflect upon times when they overcame some obstacle, felt particularly gratified by an effort or succeeded in mastering some skill or challenge. Students should not connote their "peak experience" as necessarily an "award winning" experience. It is more important that the student experienced a personal sense of mastery and satisfaction.

Students are instructed to describe three peak experiences that they have had in the past. The experiences should reflect something that they have accomplished, something they are proud they have done or some challenge that they faced in their life. The experience may be from any arena of their life such as social, artistic, physical, academic, spiritual and so on.

Three Peak Experiences

Peak Experience I

Describe the activity or event.

_____
_____
_____
_____
_____

Date of the event or your age at the time of this event.

_____

How did you become involved with the event or activity?

_____
_____
_____

What skills or attitudes were required of you to face or succeed in this event?

_____
_____
_____
_____

How did you know that this was a peak experience?

_____
_____
_____

What did you learn about yourself and others from this event or experience?

_____
_____
_____
_____
_____
_____
_____
_____
_____
_____

Peak Experience II

Describe the activity or event.

_____

_____

_____

_____

_____

Date of the event or your age at the time of the event.

_____

How did you become involved with this event or activity?

_____

_____

_____

What attitudes or skills were required of you to succeed or face this event?

_____

_____

_____

How did you know that this was a peak experience?

_____

_____

_____

What did you learn about yourself and others from this event or experience?

_____

_____

_____

_____

_____

_____

_____

_____

_____

_____

Peak Experience III

Describe the activity or event.

_____
_____
_____
_____
_____

Date of the event or your age at the time of the event.

_____

How did you become involved with this event or activity?

_____
_____
_____
_____

What attitudes and skills were required of you to succeed or face this event?

_____
_____
_____

How did you know that this was a peak experience?

_____
_____
_____

What did you learn about yourself and others from this experience?

_____
_____
_____
_____
_____
_____
_____
_____
_____

An overview of your experiences.

Are there any themes that you see in all of the peak experiences? Are there any shared causes and effects of the peak experiences?

_____

_____

_____

_____

_____

_____

_____

_____

_____

_____

Option III - Feedback from Others

This activity encourages students to consider their interests and abilities by soliciting the feedback of others. Students receive three viewpoints from three different people they know. This exercise may be even more meaningful if students select three different people who have observed them under very different circumstances. For example, students could request feedback from a friend, from someone who is just getting to know them and from a teacher, coach or employer.

1. Name of personal reference and their relationship to you.

_____

Three personal strengths that the reference sees in you.

_____

_____

_____

Three challenge areas that the reference sees for you.

_____

_____

_____

Other observations that the reference made about you.

_____

_____

_____

2. Name of personal reference and their relationship to you.

_____

Three personal strengths the reference sees in you.

_____

_____

_____

Three challenge areas that the reference sees for you.

_____

_____

_____

Other observations that the reference made about you ._____

_____

_____

3. Name of the personal reference and their relationship to you.

_____

Three personal strengths that the reference sees in you.

_____

_____

_____

Three personal challenge areas that the reference sees for you.

_____

_____

_____

Other observations that the reference made about you.

_____

_____

_____

After completing three interviews, write down some of the patterns that you noted. Were there similarities between the references? Were there any surprises that you did not anticipate? What feedback was good to hear from others?

_____

_____

_____

_____

_____

_____

_____

_____

_____

_____

Option IV - Class Partners

Unlike high school, college students are in a situation where they have different people in each of their classes and may only see their faculty in the classroom. This activity encourages students to identify a class partner for each of their courses. A class partner is very beneficial when a student misses a class and needs to get the lecture notes or in case there is a need for a clarification of a concept or assignment. Some class partners may also be very good for study support and exam preparation. Particularly commuting students can experience confusion when they miss a class and are unable to get a copy of the notes, handouts or assignments A class partner offers a class contact that can be very helpful throughout the term.

Students often find that the class partner relationship works best when the partners share something in common. For example, two students from the same residence hall or two older adult learners may make a good choice for a class partnership. A class partner relationship works best if it is established early in the term. This allows for some clarification of expectations and the opportunity to become acquainted before the pressures of the academic term mount.

Class Partners

Identify one student in each of your classes to establish a class partner relationship with so that the two of you can provide each other with support and information. This can be particularly beneficial whenever one of you misses a class or is unclear about a concept in a class.

(1) Name of Class _____

    Partner's Name _____
    Partner's Address _____
    Partner's Mail Drop or E-Mail Number _____
    Partner's Phone Number _____
    Partner's class and work schedule for the term

    _____
    _____

    Three things I have in common with my partner.
    _____

    Three ways my partner and I are different.
    _____

(2) Name of Class _____
    Partner's Name _____
    Partner's Address _____
    Partner's Mail Drop or E-Mail Number _____
    Partner's Phone Number _____
    Partner's class and work schedule for the term.

    _____
    _____

    Three things I have in common with my partner.
    _____

    Three ways my partner and I are different.
    _____

(3) Name of Class _____
    Partner's Name _____
    Partner's Address _____
    Partner's Mail Drop or E-Mail Number _____
    Partner's Phone Number _____
    Partner's class and work schedule for the term.

    _____
    _____
    _____

Three things that I have in common with my partner.

_____

Three ways that my partner and I are different.

_____

(4) Name of Class_____

    Partner's Name_____

    Partner's Address_____

    Partner's Mail Drop or E-Mail Number_____

    Partner's Phone Number_____

    Partner's class and work schedule for the term.

    _____

    _____

    _____

Three things that I have in common with my partner.

_____

Three ways that my partner and I are different.

_____

Classroom Activities

During the first week or so of the class you may opt to have students spend some class time becoming better acquainted with one another and exploring the ideas in Chapter 1. Spending some class time building a sense of class community promotes a better sense of commitment to the class and a reassurance to each student that they are not "alone" in their fears and concerns about "making the grade" in college.

Option I -Getting Acquainted

Class stands or sits in a circle so that all students can see one another. One student is asked to introduce himself or herself by first name.

Example: "Hi, my name is John".

Then the student next to John introduces his or her first name and the name of the previous student.

Example: "My name is Mary Lou and this is John".

Then the third person in the circle introduces his or her name and the names of all of the previously introduced students.

Example: "My name is Jacob and this is Mary Lou and this is John".

This process continues until the last student who must introduce himself or herself as well as all of the students who have already introduced themselves. Students are generally very willing to volunteer for this activity because they do not want to be the last student and therefore responsible to introduce all of the other students in the class.

When this activity is completed, it is often useful to process the memory tools that individual students used to help them remember the names of their classmates. By asking the individual students how they recalled the names and which names were the easiest to remember, the instructor can introduce concepts about how the brain remembers new information. Generally, students tend to recall the unusual, colorful names like Shannon, LaVonne or Leroy. Or they will remember names of students who have the same name or look like someone they know. Or students will remember the names of students who have the same name as some famous people like Marlon, Elvis or Shakespeare. This can be a helpful introduction to the learning strategies that will be discussed later in the course.

Option II - Dyads and Triads

This activity offers students the opportunity to get acquainted with one another in dyads and triads. The exercise may be more comfortable for students that may initially be a little more reserved around large groups of people. Student get together in a dyad and triad for 5-10 minutes. Each student has 2-3 minutes to share information about himself or herself with the other student(s) in the dyad or triad. After all of the students have introduced themselves within the dyad or triad, then each student introduces one of the other members of their dyad or triad to the rest of the class. Each student should give the name of student he or she is introducing as well as two or three interesting pieces of information about the student who is being introduced.

Option III - Values Mingling

This class activity encourages students to physically move around the classroom and make initial contacts with a number of different students.

Students begin by standing up and moving to the area of the classroom that has posted a value statement that they believe best depicts their beliefs and preferences. Once the student has moved to the section of the classroom that has the statement that best captures their feelings, the student is asked to introduce himself or herself to someone else in the same values grouping. Students should offer their name and why the value statement best describes their preference or opinion.

Value Statements - Selection A

To rejuvenate myself, I like to do something active.

To rejuvenate myself, I like to do something social.

To rejuvenate myself, I like to get off on my own.

Value Statements - Selection B

College is a great place to learn about new ideas.

College is a great place to meet many different types of people.

College is a great place to learn new skills for an interesting career.

College is a great place to learn facts and information.

Value Statements - Selection C

In my future career, I want to help others.

In my future career, I want stimulation and challenge

In my future career, I want to have leadership responsibilities.

In my future career, I want to express my creative side.

Personal Journaling

Each chapter contains several reflection questions that are intended to facilitate student self-awareness and personal meaning-making. There are a variety of ways that you as the instructor can use these journaling questions. First, you can give the students a reflection question at the beginning or end of a class period. Students could either keep a running journal of their thoughts throughout the term, or you may wish to collect the journal entries and review what the students have written. This can be an excellent way for you to get to know the class individually and collectively. Third, you may direct the students to share their latest journal entries with another classmate or in small groups. This can facilitate a feeling of reassurance and support between the students. The students can then also offer helpful suggestions to one another about how they have dealt with a similar concern.

You may want to use some or all of the reflection questions that are offered. On the other hand, you may also choose to write other reflection questions that more specifically meet the needs of your students.

How did you know that you wanted to come to college?

What are some of the obstacles that you have had to overcome to get to college?

What has happened since you arrived on the campus that has <u>confirmed</u> your decision to pursue higher education?

What has happened since you arrived on the campus that <u>challenged</u> your decision to pursue higher education? How did you face the challenge?

What is your greatest concern about succeeding at this college or university?

How can I as your instructor best support your goals and academic success?

Evaluating Student Mastery and Application

Exams are one way of evaluating students' progress in class but there are also other options for assessment of students' learning in the class. One example of how you can conduct a periodic check of mastery is to ask one to three questions about the previous lecture or chapter at the beginning of a class session. Students can also discuss their responses in dyads or triads. You may want to collect their answers or summary statements as a way to take attendance and also to check whether the material is clear to the students.

The following sample questions may be useful in constructing exams or tests.

Objective Test Questions

1. The fastest growing student population from 1982 to 1992 was
    a. African Americans
    b. Hispanics
    c. Asian Americans/Pacific Islanders
    d. Native Americans or Alaskan Natives
    e. Caucasians

2. Which of the characteristics is not true of students enrolled in colleges and universities today?
    a. More than 75% of the students are enrolled in four-year universities.
    b. There has been a significant increase in the number of women students attending institutions of higher learning.
    c. Most students are eager to get into the job market and therefore complete their baccalaureate degree in less than four years.
    d. About half of all college or university students are enrolled full time.
    e. a. and c.
    f. a. and d.

3. Generally, individuals who continue their education experience the most significant boost in income level at what educational attainment level?
    a. Between those who have some high school and those who have their high school degree.
    b. Between those who have their high school degree and those who have some college.
    c. Between those who have some college and those who have a college degree.
    d. Between those who have their Bachelor's degree and those who have completed their Master's degree.

4. The computer information resource that allows you to access archives and move files from other computers to your own is
   a. E-Mail
   b. Usenet
   c. Gopher
   d. FTP
   e. World-Wide Web

5. Students can become more effective as learners if they
   a. Keep an open mind.
   b. Build in rewards for themselves when they accomplish their goals.
   c. Actively engage with the class room information and ask questions of themselves and others.
   d. Ask for assistance when they are in need of support or information.

6. Which descriptive statement about adult learners is not true?
   a. The majority are married and have dependents.
   b. This population is likely to decline over the next decade.
   c. Most adult learners attend school part-time.
   d. Almost half of the adult learners work full time.

7. Students who experience fear about their college experience should
   a. Minimize their concerns because they are not typical for new college students.
   b. Seek out assistance from someone they trust.
   c. Identify the source of their fears.
   d. Consider modifying their plans and goals.
   e. Two of the above.
   f. All of the above.

8. The Internet system does not
   a. Use a network of individual computers linked through telephone technology.
   b. Allow the individual to list messages and inquiries.
   c. Contain "Home Pages" compiled by companies, schools and organizations.
   d. Offer a well-organized, documented system that the user can easily manage.

9. Education at a university or college offers the student
   a. More options for future choices.
   b. Tools for solving problems.
   c. Greater job security in general.
   d. A chance to test personal strengths.
   e. All of the above.

10. The Counseling Center on this campus (circle all that you believe are correct)
    a. Charges a fee for counseling sessions.
    b. Offers evening appointments.
    c. Conducts group and individual sessions.
    d. None of the above.

Short Answer and Essay Questions

Briefly describe three key differences between the college students of 100 years ago and the students currently enrolled in colleges and universities.

_____

_____

_____

_____

_____

What are the benefits of a college education besides getting into a job or profession?

_____

_____

_____

_____

_____

What are the personal skills and attitudes that students need in order to be successful in achieving their educational goals?

_____

_____

_____

_____

_____

What has been most meaningful for you thus far in the course? Give examples to support your answer.

_____

_____

_____

_____

_____

Key for Objective Test Questions.

1. b.
2. e.
3. d.
4. d.
5. e.
6. b.
7. e.
8. d.
9. c.
10. **Answer depends on local campus Counseling Center**

References

Astin, Alexander (1993). *What Matters in College*. San Francisco, CA.: Jossey-Bass Publishers.

Bridges, W. (1980). *Transitions*. New York: Addison-Wesley Publishing Company.

Brookfield, S. (1990). *The Skilled Teacher*. San Francisco: Jossey-Bass Publishers.

Covey, S. (1989). *The Seven Habits of Highly Effective People*. New York: Simon and Schuster.

McCarthy, M. (1991). *Mastering the Information Age*. Los Angeles: Jeremy P. Tarcher. Inc.

Pascarella, Ernest T. & Terenzini, Patrick T. (1991). *How College Effects Students*. San Francisco, CA.: Jossey-Bass Publishers.

Films for Class Use.

Film clips from the following could be useful for stimulating class discussion.

Dead Poets Society
> *1989 film distributed by Touchstone Home Video.*
> *Scenes with students and teacher engaging in lively classroom discussion could be used to explore the value and joy of learning.*

The Paper Chase
> *1973 film distributed by Twentieth Century Fox Video.*
> *Opening scene of intimidating Harvard Law Professor grilling his students could provoke discussion on fears and concerns about coming to college.*

Self-Awareness - Knowing How You Learn
Chapter 2

Key Concepts: This chapter offers a variety of tools designed to encourage and enhance students' understanding of themselves. Generally, the more students understand their particular strengths and challenges, the better able they will be to make informed choices and develop their skills and goals.

Additional Ideas to Explore with Students: Most college students are in the midst of major transitions and many life decisions. Understanding their strengths and challenges can be important information for students to consider as they make academic and career decisions. While there are many ways that learning style and individual differences have been examined, there is universal acceptance that there are characteristics unique to each person.

Medical and mental health professionals have observed variability between infants shortly after birth. One such variability is temperament. Some babies are "easy" babies because they are responsive to care and nurturing and generally socially interactive with those around them. Other babies have been identified as "slow to warm up" due to their more reticent and reserved nature. Sometimes "slow to warm up" babies will go through periods when they only want to be around their parents or someone they know very well. And still other babies have been labeled as "difficult" babies that tend to be more temperamental and high strung. (Needless to say, "difficult" babies can be a real challenge for new parents). As we grow older, the differences in interests, talents and temperament between individuals becomes more evident and generally more consistent.

For many young adults, college offers an excellent opportunity for self exploration. Within the context of a family unit, many students have come to view themselves through the "lenses" of family expectations and interests. Self awareness can maximize a student's efforts and facilitate a clearer sense of purpose for attending college. As the student becomes more aware of his or her learning style and abilities, it is important to stress that there is no best way of being or learning. However, different abilities and attitudes may be an easier "fit" to certain types of tasks. In general, the majority of students will experience some level of discrepancy between their preferred learning style and the type of learning that is expected within institutions of higher learning.

Besides the learning style inventory that is included in the text book, there are a number of other helpful inventories that may be helpful to include in class time. If you are not familiar with some of the inventories, you may want to seek out staff from your university's Counseling Center or from the Career Development and Placement Office. The following list of additional inventories may be ones that you will want to consider.

Strong Vocational Inventory. This instrument is based on the vocational model developed by Holland. Six typologies are used to assist individuals in exploring various career paths. Holland offers the six types that include Realistic, Artistic, Social, Intellectual, Entrepreneurial, and Conservative. If you are interested in pursuing materials on the Strong Vocational Inventory, mail your inquiry to Consulting Psychologists Press, Inc., 3803 E. Bayshore Road, Palo Alto, CA. 94303.

Myers-Briggs Type Inventory (MBTI). The MBTI is a self-report assessment tool based on the psychological theory of Carl Jung (1875-1961). Jung believed that individuals have natural preferences that shape their perspectives and approaches to life. Four scales are delineated in the MBTI that include the following: Perceiving vs. Judging, Sensing vs. Intuition, Thinking vs. Feeling, and Introversion vs. Extroversion.. The MBTI and additional materials can be purchased from Consulting Psychologist Press Inc., 3803 East Bayshore Road, Palo Alto, CA. 94303.

Gregorc Adult Style Inventory. A self-assessment instrument for adults that reveals mental qualities and mediation channels that individuals utilize to learn and interact with others. The inventory explores two primarily matrixes -- Time and Space. The Time dimension refers to how one organizes oneself to accomplish tasks and goals. The Space dimension explores the source of one's ideas and realities. Copies of the inventory can be ordered by writing to Gregorc Associates, Inc., 15 Doubleday Road, Box 351, Columbia, CT. 06237-9975.

4MAT. A learning style assessment that was developed by Bernice McCarthy in 1986. Using the left and right brain approaches for processing information and ideas, this instrument can be very helpful to the instructor who wants to appeal to different types of learners. More information can be acquired from The Learning Style Inventory, Tests and Scoring Division, McBer and Company, Boston, MA.

"Discover" Computer Search. An interactive career exploration software package that includes one section on learning about oneself. This computer program allows students to prioritize their values and interests. Annual licensing fees are required. If interested, write to American College Testing, Educational Technology Center-East, 230 Schilling Circle, Suite 350, Hunt Valley, Maryland 21031.

Individual Assignments

Option I - Assessing Your Classes for Learning Style Preference

Gather all of the syllabi that you have received in your current classes. Look for key words, phrases and assignments that give you indications about the learning style preference(s) that are going to be particularly useful in each class. For example, an assignment like a "Class presentation with a group from the class" strongly utilizes the "Active" and "Verbal" learning styles. Now go through your current syllabi and identify the key words and then identify what learning style preferences might be needed to achieve the class expectations.

Use the learning style preferences identified in the textbook on pages 42-47.

Class Name:_____

Key Word(s)	Learning Style Preference
a._____	_____
b._____	_____
c._____	_____
d._____	_____
e._____	_____

Class Name:_____

Key Word(s)	
a._____	_____
b._____	_____
c._____	_____
d._____	_____
e._____	_____

Class Name:_____

Key Word(s)	
a._____	_____
b._____	_____
c._____	_____
d._____	_____
e._____	_____

Knowing what you do about your own learning style, describe which class will probably be the most comfortable match for your learning style preferences and why.

_____

_____

_____

_____

_____

Which class will probably be the greatest challenge for your learning style and why? What specific activities and attitudes can you use to compensate for any learning style challenge that you have?

_____

_____

_____

_____

_____

Option II - Autobiography of You as a Learner

This self-reflection paper can be an excellent way for students to gain some objectivity about their own experiences as a learner and the ways that those experiences have shaped their perceptions and self-confidence. Additionally, these papers frequently give faculty members valuable insights into the lives of students.

Students are to write about the experiences and relationships that have been influential to their perceptions of how they learn, how they view themselves as learners and what motivates them. A variation on this approach is to have students describe in writing their three most important learning experiences or relationships and to speculate on what the three reveal about the way they learn best and what motivates them. The paper should be 3-5 pages in length and should highlight approximately 3-5 significant experiences that have impacted how they view themselves as learners. This paper should not be a chronicle of every teacher they have had or school they have attended. Instead the paper should focus on pivotal experiences from their childhood to their college education.

Frequently, students may still be somewhat unclear about what to include in their paper, so it may be helpful to give some illustrations or to have the class brainstorm some examples. The following represents some suggestions to facilitate class discussion: expectations of parents, a learning or physical disability, frequently changing schools while they were growing up, a divorce or marital separation, a particularly gifted brother or sister, an encouraging teacher or coach, etc..
Students should include specific examples and should connect their experiences and relationships to a specific belief or attitude that they have about themselves as learners in college. Papers should identify learning strengths as well as challenges.

Option III - Personal Assessment: Getting to Know Myself as a Learner

In my environment, I can concentrate best when...

1. The sound level is
    ___High
    ___Medium
    ___Low

    and _____ music is playing.

    I can hear the sounds of
    ___People
    ___Traffic
    ___Other_____

2. The light is
    ___Bright
    ___Medium
    ___Low

    The light is
    ___Artificial
    ___Natural

3. The temperature is
    ___Cool
    ___Medium
    ___Warm

4. The room is
    ___Open
    ___Structured
    ___Non-structured

5. The ideal environment for me to study in is_____.

6. On this campus, this environment is located_____.

7. I like to study

       ___Alone

       ___Alone but in the presence of others

       ___In a group

8. I learn best by

       ___Reading about something

       ___Hearing something

       ___Experiencing something (hands on)

       ___Seeing something on tape or film

9. I am motivated by (Rank from 1-5)

       ___My sense of accomplishment

       ___Competing against others

       ___Encouragement from authority persons

       ___Tangible rewards

       ___Sense of team work with others

       ___Approval of family and friends

       ___Long term goals

       ___Seeing what I can achieve at an excellent level

       ___Other_____

Option IV - Changing a Habit

Think about one personal habit that you would like to eliminate.

1. Why is this habit troublesome for you? How is this habit negatively influencing your current lifestyle? Is this habit inhibiting you from accomplishing some positive goals that you have for yourself?

_____

_____

_____

_____

2. What "rewards" does continuing this habit offer to you?

_____

_____

3. What specifically do you want to accomplish with regard to this goal within the next month? Example: "I want to lose three pounds." or "I want to complete all of my assignments three hours before they are due." or "I want to watch one hour of television per day."

_____

_____

_____

4. What one thing can you do today that will get you on the road to changing or eliminating a particular habit?

_____

_____

5. Who can be an individual that you can report to and that will support you in changing or eliminating this habit? _____

6. How will you reward yourself if you achieve your goal for changing or eliminating a habit at the end of the month period?

_____

_____

_____

Classroom Activities

Option I - Buying an Automobile

This activity is designed to facilitate students' understanding and appreciation for individual differences as distinguished by the Learning Style Inventory offered in the textbook. Students are instructed to pretend that they are about to purchase a new car. How will they determine which car to buy? How will they gather information about the quality, safety and cost of the car? What criterion do they have for the car that they want to purchase? What steps do they take to make this purchase?

Next, divide students into groups based upon their scores on the learning style scales in the textbook. Ask students who have a score of "5" or higher on the Active Scale to form a small group and those students with a score of "5" or higher on the Reflective Scale to form another small group. The remainder of the class become observers with half sitting around the Reflective group and the other half sitting around the Active group. As observers, their role is to make notations and listen for the problem-solving strategies used by the two groups. Now give 5-10 minutes to the two groups to discuss how they would go about purchasing an automobile. After the groups have finished discussing their steps for selecting a car, the observer groups will highlight what they heard as they listened to the Active or Reflective group. Have a recorder write on the chalk or white board what the observers share. Are there differences in the groups? What considerations did one group have that the other group did not? What do these differences tell us about the learning style of each of these groups? What might be some special strengths and challenges for each of these learning style approaches?

You may want to establish two other small discussion groups based on one of the other learning style preferences that is Sensing vs. Intuitive, Visual vs. Verbal or Sequential vs. Global. Once again, the observers would be utilized to note the differences in processing for the two groups. Instead of the automobile purchase, the groups could discuss how they would select a college or prepare for a vacation.

Option II - Case Study

Divide the students into groups of approximately five individuals each. The group should select a recorder who will share a summary of the group's discussion.

Case Study. You are the Director of Personnel at a small advertising company. The atmosphere is very creative and energetic. While the business has generally been very successful, you as the Director of Personnel has noted that the employees are not very good with details and accounting reports. Today you must determine whom you will hire for the position of Business Manager.

What learning style preferences do you believe would be advantageous to look for the applicants for this new staff addition? Explain why you believe these learning style preferences would be helpful to the company.

Option III - The Party

This activity is a simple, yet fairly effective vehicle for promoting self-awareness and an appreciation of individual differences. Students are asked to stand up and move into groupings with other students who share their same choice at a "party mixer." Groupings will be conducted three times. Using the diagram that follows, ask students to move to the corner or place in the room that would be their first choice. You may want to tape signs on the classroom walls so students know where to move. After the students have "mingled" with other students who are in their same cluster, they will be asked to move into a second grouping that is different from the first. This selection should represent the group of people that they would be most comfortable with if everyone from the first group left the party. Repeat this process for a third grouping.

When the three groupings have been completed, ask students to return to their seats. Then process the activity as a class. Are there some dominant groupings in the class? Did a majority of the students join one or two groups? What might these trends indicate about the makeup of this class? Were there any students who moved from group to group together? Were there any students who never shared the same grouping with them?

THE PARTY

A circular diagram divided into six segments, with "People Who:" in the center circle.

I = like to observe, investigate, analyze, evaluate, or solve problems.

R = have mechanical ability, prefer to work with objects, machines, tools, plants

A = have artistic, innovative, or intuitional abilities, and like situations using imagination and creativity.

C = like to work with data, have clerical or numeric ability, carrying things out in detail or following through on other's instruction.

S = like to work with people-to inform, enlighten, help, train, develop, or cure them, or are skilled with words.

E = like to work with people-influencing, persuading, performing, for organizational goals or economic gain.

1

Which corner of the room would you be instinctively drawn to as the group of people you would most enjoy being with for the longest time? (Leave aside any questions of shyness, or whether you would have to talk with them.) Write your letter from the corner here:

2

After fifteen minutes, everyone in the corner you have chosen, left to another party across town, except you. Of the groups that still remain, which group would you be drawn to the the most, as people you would most enjoy being with the longest time? Write the letter from the corner here:

3

After fifteen minutes, this group also leaves for another party except you. Of the remaining groups, which one would you most enjoy being with for the longest time? Write the letter from the corner here:

34

Journaling Activities

What learning style did I observe in my parents? How did they seem to validate my learning style? What, if any, were some ways that my parents did not seem to understand or validate my learning style?

How do I see my natural learning style preferences matching with the career(s) that I am currently considering? What career responsibilities might be stressful or a stretch for me in terms of my learning style preferences?

Do I tend to strike up friendships with people who have learning styles that are more similar or different from me? Have I ever experienced a teacher or supervisor who did not appear to appreciate my learning style?

How is my best friend or significant other like me or different than me?. What learning style do I see in them? How does that match or not match my own learning style?

Evaluating Student Mastery and Application
Chapter 2

Objective Test Questions

1. Which of the following is an example of positive self-talk?
   a. I will try to get an "A" in my Sociology class.
   b. I have to get on the varsity team.
   c. I will make new friends in my residence hall.
   d. I should be losing some weight and getting into better shape.

2. An Active learner tends to learn best by
   a. Getting into study groups and explaining the class information to others.
   b. Writing journal entries about what is being learned in a class.
   c. Considering the meaning and relevance of the material being covered in a class.
   d. Doing an internship and learning on the job.
   e. a. and d.
   f. a. and b.

3. A Global learner tends not to
   a. Accomplish tasks with a clear, step by step procedure.
   b. See the individual parts of project prior seeing the overall concept or goal.
   c. Learn individual, isolated facts easily.
   d. Be aware of the physical space and belongings.
   e. All of the above.

4. A student who learns best by getting together with a study group is using what learning style preference?
   a. Global
   b. Reflective
   c. Sensing
   d. Verbal

5. A state of mind or disposition is a(an)
   a. Habit
   b. Attitude
   c. Learning Style
   d. Self-concept
   e. Self-Confidence

Short Answer and Essay Questions

1. Assume that you have a roommate who is very strong in the following learning style preferences: Global, Verbal, Intuitive and Reflective. When it comes to studying, will this roommate be an effective study partner for you? First, indicate your learning style preference and then highlight specific ways that you and your roommate might help or hinder one another while studying. What challenges might there be for you living with this person? What way might this roommate be a good match for you? Be specific.

_____
_____
_____
_____
_____
_____
_____

2. List three specific ways that you will need to adapt or enhance your learning style to succeed in college. Be specific.

_____
_____
_____
_____
_____
_____

3. Explain how a person with a strong Global Learning Style would differ from a person with a strong Sequential Learning Style when learning a new job.

_____
_____
_____
_____
_____
_____
_____

Key to Objective Test Questions

1. c.
2. e.
3. e.
4. d.
5. b.

References

Bolles, Richard Nelson (1991). *The 1990 What Color is Your Parachute*? Berkeley, CA.: Consolidated Printers, Inc..

Carter, Carol (1990). *Majoring in theRest of Your Life*. New York: Noonday Press.

Clawson, James G., Kotter, John P., Faux, Victor A. & McArthur (1992). *Self-Assesment and Career Development*. Cliffs, N.J.: Prentice-Hall, Inc..

Gregorc, Anthony (1985). *Inside styles*. Maynard, MA.: Gabriel Systems, Inc..

Lawrence, Gordon (1993). *People Types and Tiger Stripes*. Ocala, FL.: Special Publications Inc..

Morris, Susan & McCarthy, Bernice (1990). *4MAT*. Barrington, IL.: EXCEL, Inc..

Myers, Isabel (1980). *Gifts Differing*. Palo Alto, CA.: Consulting Psychologists Press Inc..

Mapping Your Course:
Goals, Priorities and Time Management
Chapter 3

Key Concepts: Time management is clearly one of the most challenging aspects of college for most new students. Increased freedom, less supervision and new educational demands create pressures for students that they do not generally have skills to meet effectively. Often students are eager for "quick fixes" that will assist them in managing their time. However, it is much more difficult to assist students in thoughtfully defining their goals and personal mission. The familiar exchange between the Cheshire Cat and Alice (in Wonderland) captures the students' dilemma of trying to go somewhere but not knowing their destination.

> "Cheshire Puss," she began, rather timidly, as she did not at all know whether it would like the name; however, it only grinned a little wider. "Come, it's pleased so far," thought Alice, and she went on. "Would you tell me, please, which way I ought to go from here?"
> "That depends a good deal on where you want to get to," said the Cat.
> "I don't much care where-" said Alice.
> "Then it doesn't matter which way you go," said the Cat.

<u>Alice in Wonderland</u>
By Carrol Lewis

Additional Ideas to Explore with Students: One of the greatest challenges about time management is making choices. By taking some time to clarify goals, both long term and short term, students will have a frame of reference for making the day by day decisions that they encounter. In addition, many students have not made personal decisions that reflect what they value and want to achieve. Instead, their goals reflect what their parents and peers consider important.

After goal setting has been explored, students will also need practical strategies for maximizing their time and becoming assertive so that other people do not shape their commitments. In addition, it is critical for students to learn how to structure a good working space and how to complete major projects in a timely fashion. The following strategies may be helpful to include in the class lectures and discussions.

<u>Organizing One's Environment</u>
The systems that students develop to organize their working and living space can make a significant difference in their educational confidence and achievement. First, students need to consider their office or work space in terms of what objects are most important and useful. It is helpful to place those things that they will need every day or so within "arm's length" when they are sitting at their desk. Things that will be needed every two to seven days can be stored in places that are three to six feet farther away than that arm's stretch. In

other words, the things that the students need most frequently should be stored closest to their desk chair. Second, students should make a decision about how to organize their files. How long and where to keep course syllabi, bills, income tax forms, insurance policies and registration information are decisions that students are addressing for the first time. Processing how to make such decisions for storing documents and paperwork is an important concept to guide students through.

Scheduling Activities

Because students are juggling many different responsibilities and activities, a Master Calendar can be a very helpful strategy. Essentially, a Master Calendar is the consolidation of all assignments, appointments and activities on one calendar. This allows students to "see" all the commitments that they are facing on a "one-stop" calendar.

Processing Paper

Despite the use of E-Mail and the various computer programs, students receive many handouts, mail, magazines, syllabi and other documents that become very unwieldy. Making decisions about what to do with each piece of "paper" as soon possible is one constructive step in managing the deluge of paper information. Essentially, students have only a limited number of options about what to do with the paper. It can be tossed, sent on to someone else, filed or acted upon. The sooner students can learn to make the decision about what to do with the paper they receive, the less clutter and misplaced materials they will have to worry about.

Handling Phone Calls

For some students this is not a major issue but for many, time spent on the phone is a significant time waster. Learning how to "get off" the phone is a necessary skill that many students often do not have. Taking time in class to brainstorm techniques for handling the phone is a practical way to assist students in learning different options. Also, teaching some basic business telephone etiquette can be very useful to some students. Learning the importance of leaving their name, phone number and the nature of their call, or getting the name of one person in an office or store that is their contact person, are tools for telephone efficiency.

Handling Visitors

Many students struggle with how to establish boundaries. If they live in a residence hall, they have a difficult time knowing how to tell a friend that they are busy. If they are a parent or spouse, they do not want to disappoint a family member who is requesting time. If they live at home with their parents, they are not comfortable telling their mom or dad that they are unable to be home for dinner because they need to study at the library. Students need to learn and practice skills for how to make their commitments known and respected by those around them. Assertiveness is social skill that requires practice for many students. (See Case Study in the Classroom Activities section) In addition, students can benefit from informing those around them of their commitments and posting their calendar. Finally, scheduling frequent "Visitors" for designated and perhaps even regular appointments can take the urgency out of the drop-in visits.

Individual Assignments

Option I - Working Backwards

Working Backwards is a time-management technique that can assist students in managing long term projects so they are not scrambling at the last minute to finish an assignment such as a major term paper. Students are to select one major assignment that they have at least two to three weeks to complete like an exam, a group presentation or a research project. First, students should brainstorm all of the sub-tasks that must be done to ultimately accomplish the assignment. Parenthetically, this step is sometimes referred to as the "Swiss Cheese" technique by some time-management experts. Students are taking their big piece of "cheese" and poking holes into it.

Second, students should take their list of sub-tasks and count back the number of days from the deadline of the major assignment to today. Then the sub-tasks should be broken down to what tasks need to be accomplished week by week. Next, the student translates the weekly tasks into daily tasks and posts them on a master calendar. And finally, students should monitor their progress by checking off or highlighting the tasks on the Master Calendar as each activity is accomplished.

Example:

Step 1 - "I need to prepare for my mid-term Biology examination by November 14."

Step 2 - Brainstorm of all the sub-tasks that need to be accomplished by November 14.

      a. Read Chapter 1, 2, 3, 4, and 5
      b. Take notes, flashcards and/or summary sheets for Chapters 1-5
      c. Form a study group
      d. Schedule study sessions with the study group
      e. Meet with professor to discuss class expectations and exam strategies.
          f. Meet with tutor once weekly
      g. Review notes and prepare for exam 8 hours total

Step 3 - Determine when each of the sub-tasks listed in Step 2 will be done during the weeks prior to the deadline and then post on Master Calendar.

Option II - "To Do" List Evaluation

Write out a "To Do" list for each day for one week. Use a prioritizing system to indicate the degree of significance for each item on your "To Do" list. Use an "A" to indicate "essential" or very important to complete on that day, "B" for those items that are fairly important to complete on the particular day and "C" for those activities that would be nice to finish but not essential. ""C" do not require your immediate attention and are often small easy jobs to complete, and so these activities are the "if-there's time" type of projects. You may want to place a number after the letters to determine the order in which you plan to accomplish your daily tasks. Collect your "To Do" lists for one week and indicate what activities you accomplished on time and also what activities did not get completed on schedule. Then, on a separate sheet of paper answer the following questions. How did you feel about using a "To Do" list to get things done? Did you accomplish what you wanted to during the past week? If not, what particular projects did not get done in a timely fashion? What do you believe are the specific reasons the projects did not get done? Are there things you can do to facilitate a better record for completing your assignments and activities in an efficient and effective manner?

Sample "TO DO" List

Date_____

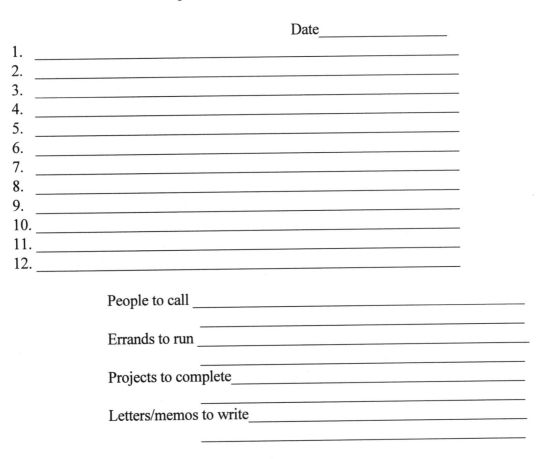

1. _____
2. _____
3. _____
4. _____
5. _____
6. _____
7. _____
8. _____
9. _____
10. _____
11. _____
12. _____

People to call _____
_____

Errands to run _____
_____

Projects to complete_____
_____

Letters/memos to write_____
_____

What projects did not get finished on schedule?_____

_____

Am I trying to do too much or not enough each day?

_____

_____

_____

_____

_____

_____

Where do I lose time each day?

_____

_____

_____

Option III - Procrastination File

For one week, monitor the activities that you procrastinate. Your "To Do" list provides you with a good place to start. Also, think about the activities that you did not include on your "To Do" list that you wanted to accomplish such as taking some quiet time to meditate or pray, or starting an exercise program, or responding to an invitation. List ten activities that you procrastinated during the last week or two. If you procrastinated more than once, indicate the number of times that you intended to engage in the activity. Then identify the main reason(s) that you procrastinated each one. Finally, review the entire "Profile" and write down your observations. Are there trends? Are there certain types of activities that you procrastinate? Do you do better completing tasks when you are alone or with others? Are you trying to make too many changes at one time?

Procrastination Profile

	Task	Reason for Procrastination
1.		
2.		
3.		
4.		
5.		
6.		
7.		
8.		
9.		
10.		

What are some of the trends that you notice in your Procrastination Profile?

_____

_____

_____

_____

_____

_____

Are there specific strategies that you can put into place that can help you deal more constructively with the activities that you tend to procrastinate such as "getting an exercise partner to work out with you each day"?

_____

_____

_____

_____

Classroom Activities

Option I - Case Studies

Divide the class into groups of five to seven individuals. Give each group a time management scenario that the group members will first discuss and then attempt to act through for the rest of the class. Their skit should include a productive resolution of the dilemma that is based on skills that they have been learning in the class. Another alternative would also be acting out the scenario and then leading a discussion with the rest of the class about some various ways that the dilemma could be resolved.

Scenario I - Group Assignment

You are a member of a five-person group project group in a class. Three of the members are working hard to have regular meetings together and divide the work load. Your professor has told you that 35% of your individual grade for the class will be determined by the group project. Two of the people in your class project group are old high school friends who have not seen each other for several years. Now they spend most of the time reminiscing over old times and joking around when they should be working with the rest of the group. In addition, the same two students do not seem to be getting their fair share of the work accomplished. What do you do?

Scenario II -- Roommate Tensions

You are resident hall roommates with a person who you really enjoy as a friend. Your roommate is much more outgoing than you are and you have met many great people because your roommate has introduced you to so many of the people she/he knows. During the first two weeks of the school term, your room was the social headquarters of the residence hall floor and you loved the energy and the excitement of the interactions. Now, however, you are becoming concerned about studying and need your room to become a quiet place for studying instead of socializing. When you bring up your concern for the first time, your roommate's response is sympathetic but nothing really changes. What do you do next?

Scenario III - Family Commitments

You are married to a great person who is currently working full time in a fairly stressful job. When you first decided to continue your college education, your spouse was very supportive. In fact, your spouse is financially supporting your education so you will only need to work for pay 15-20 hours per week. Because your spouse has not been in college, he/she does not fully appreciate the time that you need to study. In the evening, your spouse believes that the two of you should be spending time together. Your spouse believes that if he/she can do their job during the day, then you should be able to get your school work done during the day. You know that your study demands require you to study in the evenings. What do you do?

Option II - Tennis Ball Activity

This activity is a great way to get a work to experience a "metaphor" for the juggling of many time demands and responsibilities Get the class into a circle with no more than one to two feet between each student. If you have a very crowded classroom, you may choose to move the group outside of the building. Once students are in a circle, tell them to put up one hand. Then, beginning with one of the students, ask each student to toss the ball to one of the students who has his/her hand up in the air. Once the student has received that ball, he/she should put his/her hand down and pass the ball on to another student. When everyone in the class has received and tossed the ball, the last person to catch the ball should toss it back to the first person who tossed the ball.

Now that the ball has circulated to everyone, ask that the students recirculate the ball by repeating the same pattern of throwing as they did the first time. Students do not hold their hands up this second time, but if someone forgets where they threw the ball, he/she can be prompted. After everyone has received the ball again, then the ball is returned to the first student. Ask the student to repeat this process several more times getting more efficient and effective as they practice. What happens when someone misses the ball? Stop the ball throwing and discuss how well they are doing. Are there some things that could be done to improve their accuracy and speed? Have students share their ideas with one another and then using this input, return to the ball throwing using the same format. Then ask the students to reverse the order of throwing. Stop, process How well did they do? Did their speed and accuracy change? Improve? Deteriorate?

And finally, have the students return to their original pattern of throwing the tennis ball. After a minute or so, hand another tennis ball to the first student and ask them to start the throwing pattern with the second ball. There should now be two balls moving through the air. A minute or so later, add a third and perhaps, even a fourth ball. One of these balls might be different in size or texture. When the group has sent the three or four balls around the group several times; stop to share how the activity is being experienced. Are they feeling stressed out? How are they coping with the increased demands? Are they watching carefully to see that the balls do not collide? Are they becoming more directive or less directive with one another? Have some people pulled back a little? Are some members using humor to cope with the stress level? Are members focusing on only the person that they need throw to? Take time to process the activity and then explore how the "balls" might parallel work assignments in their job. Are there any parallels between how they threw the ball and how they handle their various demands?

Option III - Juggling the Balls Processing

This activity can be a good way for students to "name" the commitments and challenges in their life. Students will receive a handout that has an outline of a person juggling a number of balls. Students are asked to label the commitments that they are currently facing. What are the "balls" that they are currently juggling? After they have completed their labeling, students should get together in dyads and triads and share the "balls" that they are juggling. Do the balls feel out of control? Are there any balls that should be removed? What balls feel the most challenging? This handout can be a simple outline of a person or use the following handout.

Journaling Activities

To achieve my goals, I need to spend more time on...
and less time on...

What people or commitments are taking time and energy away from me?

At the end of the day, when I think about what I have done, I feel...

Things I am currently avoiding right now include....
Something I want to begin today is...

Evaluating Student Mastery and Application
Chapter 3

Objective Test Questions

1. According to the text book writers, goals can be organized into five categories which include the following:
    a. Personal
    b. Family
    c. Health
    d. Leisure and Recreation
    e. a. and b.
    f. a. and c.

2. "Time Traps" often hinder students from accomplishing tasks in an effective and efficient manner. Which of the following is not an example of a "Time Trap"?
    a. Studying in a distracting location
    b. Delegating to others
    c. Not thinking ahead
    d. Curbing your social time

3. Select the activity or attitude that demonstrates a shifting of your priorities.
    a. Considering your stage of life
    b. Adapting to your state of mind
    c. Responding to an emergency
    d. Adjusting to the time of year
    e. All of the above

4. Sequential, sensor learners are more likely than global learners to
    a. Develop a system for calendarizing all of their projects
    b. Tend to see the Big Picture
    c.. Need to be reminded about what needs to get done and when
    d. Get things done when the "spirit moves them"

5. A Master Calendar should include:
    a. All of your homework deadlines
    b. Dentist appointments
    c. A birthday party for your sister
    d. Exam schedule
    e. b. and c.
    f. All of the above

6. Examples of "if-there's-time-tasks" include which of the following?
   a. Alphabetizing your CD collection
   b. Studying for an exam
   c. Meeting with your academic advisor to select classes for next term
   d. Applying for financial aid

Essay and Short Answer.

1. Review the following "TO DO" list. Then describe at least three changes that would make the list a more effective time-management tool.

    TO DO LIST
Shower
Take dog to vet
Study history
Read novel for class
Meet with study group
Buy stamps
Call home
Do Calculus problems
Exercise
Make posters for publicity
Have oil changed in car
Write letter to John
Start research paper
Call advisor

_____
_____
_____
_____
_____
_____
_____

Define the following concepts and give an example, real or imaginary, or what the concept might look like.

Swiss Cheese Technique_____
_____
_____

Illustration or Example of the Concept_____
_____
_____

Lifestyle Goals_____

_____

_____

Illustration or Example of this Concept_____

_____

_____

_____

Key to Test Questions

1. e.
2. b.
3. e.
4. a.
5. e.
6. a.

The short essay response regarding the TO DO list could include any of the following observations:

1. **The list should be prioritized using A., B., and C**
2. **The list is too long**
3. **The list is too general on many items like writing the research paper**
4. **List includes showering which should not be included as an "action" item on a TO DO list**
5. **The list could be organized by scheduled times**

Instructor: Please note that the **Swiss Cheese** concept was not discussed in the textbook.

References

Barkas, J.L. (1984). *Creative Time management.* New York: Prentice Hall Press.

Csikszentmihalyi, Mihaly (1990). *Flow.*New York: Harper and Row Publishers, Inc..

Douglas, Merrill E. & Douglas, Donna N. (1993). *Manage Your Time and Your Work Yourself.* New York: AMACON.

Servan-Schreiber, Jean-Louis (1988). *The Art of Time.* New York: Addison Wesley Publishing Company, Inc..

Winston, Stephanie (1978). *Getting Organized.* New York: Warner Books Edition.

Opening Doors: Thinking Critically and Creatively
Chapter 4

Key Concepts: With expanded technology and computer access, the challenge for students is no longer locating information. More than ever, today's students need to become critical thinkers equipped to reflect on the *quality* and *meaning* of information. This chapter focuses on the critical thinking skills and creative problem-solving approaches that are expected in the academic setting as well as the world of work.

Additional Ideas to Explore with Students: Students making the transition from high school to college are frequently surprised by the academic expectations that require them to think more deeply about ideas and information. For many students, memorizing facts was sufficient for their academic success during high school. As university and college students, they are challenged to new levels of critical thinking and creative problem solving.

Critical thinking is a multi-faceted process. First, critical thinking involves making judgments about the quality and source of information and opinions. Second, critical thinking entails determining how much information is adequate for making a decision or solving a problem. Third, critical thinking actively considers ways that information and ideas can be used in new and different ways.

The accessibility of information today makes critical thinking more essential than at any point in history. There is a challenge not to become anesthetized by the deluge of information and media stimulation. Students need to do more than amass information; now they must determine the worth of the information and when the information acquired is sufficient to achieve their purposes.

A few brief illustrations serve to demonstrate what American citizens are facing in terms of the flood of information now available to most individuals.

> *On the average, Americans see 30,000 television commercials annually (McCarthy, 1991, p. 152).

> *Daily, scientists are completing 7,000 research papers (McCarthy, 1991, p. 14).

> *Millions of words can now be stored on a five and a quarter-inch compact disc.

> *Information is currently doubling every five years but by the year 2000, information will double every 20 months.

*The half life of an engineer's knowledge today is only five years. (Certon, 1994, p.4)

*Eighty-five percent of the information in National Institutes of Health Computers is upgraded every five years. (Certon, 1994, p. 5)

College students also need to learn skills for creative collaboration and constuctive problem solving. Their future professional success will be greatly enhanced by their willingness to take risks and to view situations from different vantage points. A classroom environment that encourages experimentation and creativity provides students with the opportunities to discover their personal potential to solve future problems.

This chapter introduces the critical thinking and creative problem-solving concepts using "down-to-earth" language and examples because many college students will better be able to understand and practice the models. The Thinklink approach offers students a clear description of the different types of thinking activities that university professors expect. You may decide to include an introduction to other more abstract approaches to understanding thinking like Bloom's Taxonomy or the principles of deductive and inductive reasoning.

This chapter's focus on critical thinking and creative problem solving are aptly captured by Jean Piaget in the following quote. "The principal goal of education is to create men (and women) who are capable of doing new things, not simply of repeating what other generations have done - men (and women) who are creative, inventive and are discovers. The second goal of education is to form minds which can be critical, can verify, and not accept everything that is offered."

Individual Assignments

Option I - Reviewing the Media

Students should watch either "Meet the Press" or a news show like "Sixty Minutes" on television. As they watch one of the featured stories presented on the show, they should take notes on the information and ideas that are presented. They should label the information presented by the commentator or interviewee according to the mind actions from the Thinktrix.

<u>Illustrations:</u>

*Does the news story focus on one person's story to generalize about a larger population that may share a similar story or situation?

*Is a value judgement about an issue evident in the news presentation?

*What evidence did the commentator or newscaster use to make their point?

*What was the main point of the news presentation?

Students should attempt to record at least one illustration or example of each type of mind actions from the Thinktrix Model on page 83 of the textbook. See next page for a work sheet students can follow.

Thinktrix Analysis

Name of television show viewed

_____

Date of show_____

Recall

Similarity

Difference

Cause and Effect

Example to Idea

Idea to Example

Evaluation

Classroom Activities

Option I - Brainstorming Activity

Many students have limited experience with a group brainstorming activity. This activity introduces students to the basic steps of creative brainstorming.

Students assemble in groups with five to eight members. Each group should select a recorder whose job is to record all of the ideas generated regardless of the quality or feasibility. Groups will have 10-15 minutes to generate as many creative ideas as possible. The following principles should guide their brainstorming session.

1. No ideas are too crazy or ridiculous.
2. The goal is quantity of ideas not quality.
3. Group members can "piggy back" on one another's ideas but they should not discount the ideas offered by others in the group.
4. No idea can be put down or criticized because the idea has been tried before or failed previously or doesn't seem to fit.
5. If the group appears to slow down or become quiet during the brainstorming, the members should not assume they have run out of ideas. This reflective period may be precursory to the most creative responses.

Once this process has been explained, each group will be given a topic or focus for their brainstorming. Depending upon how much time you wish to devote to this activity, you may want to use the "Improved Products/Gadgets" options as well as the "Making Changes at the University" options.

A. New or Improved Products/Gadgets

1. How could you improve on a two-wheel bike?

2. How could you improve on the standard back pack?

3. How could you improve on the standard television set?

B. Making Changes on the University Campus

1. How can you improve on the campus policies for grading, registration? Billings?

2. How can the campus food service be improved?

3. What could the university do to make the campus more "student friendly"?

After the small groups have brainstormed, have each group prioritize the best or most ingenious ideas. Then have someone from each group post their five best ideas on the chalk board or white board. Spend some time discussing the process that each group experienced. Was it difficult to not criticize the ideas that were generated? Was it risky to share an idea that might seem foolish or outrageous to others? Did one idea lead to another even more exciting possibility?

If some intriguing ideas are offered by the groups related to the campus improvements, it might be worthwhile to collect all of the ideas and pass them along to the appropriate office or department on campus. For example, passing along the suggestions for improvements with the Campus Food Service to the Food Service Department may give that staff some helpful ideas. Also, this will affirm the creative efforts of the students.
This can create the beginning of a communication link between two constituencies on the campus.

Option II - Application for ThinkTrix

Using the children's classic, <u>Alexander's Horrible, Terrible, Awful, No Good Very Bad Day</u> by Judith Voist can be an upbeat way to reinforce the critical thinking skills outlined in the ThinkTrix information in the <u>Keys to Success</u> textbook (p.83). First, read <u>Alexander</u> out loud to the entire class. Overheads of the pictures could be made from the book so the students can follow along as you read. If you have a student who has a gift for public speaking or dramatics, you might invite him/her to be the story book reader. Some students may recall this familiar story from their childhood and may even chime in on the refrain, "It has been a terrible, awful, no good, very bad day."

After you have completed the story, distribute the following "quiz" and ask the students to answer the "test" questions.

More important than the actual "correctness" of the students' answers to these questions is the understanding of what thinking activity is being asked for in each of the questions. So, as you are giving the "correct" answers, take the time to process what mind activity is being used from the Thinktrix to answer each question.

QUIZ
for
<u>Alexander's Horrible, Terrible, Awful, No Good, Very Bad Day</u>

1. Paul's best friend is
    a. Albert Moyo
    b. Phillip Parker
    c. Bill Smith
    d. Alexander

2. The vegetable that Alexander hates is
    a. Green Beans
    b. Lima Beans
    c. Squash
    d. Spinach

3. Short essay. Alexander's older brother, Theodore, is having a day that is similar to that of Alexander. What hypothetical events do you believe Theodore might be experiencing on campus?

_____

_____

_____

4. What Biblical character most closely parallels Alexander's experience?
    a. Solomon
    b. Job
    c. Paul
    d. John

5. Based on the pattern of events of this day, what might Alexander predict would happen to him while he is sleeping?
    a. His parents check in on him while he is sleeping.
    b. His brothers leave him a present under his bed.
    c. He has pleasant dreams and wakes up refreshed.
    d. His dog eats his favorite baseball mit.

6. Alexander's Dad told Alexander not to come back to the office because of Alexander's behavior. Alexander's Dad is basing his concern about Alexander using what "Mind Action" from the Thinktrix? In other words, how is his Dad thinking?
    a. Categorization
    b. Rating
    c. Genealization
    d. Consequence
    e. Description

7. Essentially, Alexander's Mom is suggesting that Alexander handle his difficult day in accordance with which of these proverbs?
    a. "A stitch in time saves nine." Ben Franklin
    b. "The only thing we have to fear is fear itself." Winston Churchill
    c. "Behind every cloud is a silver lining." Unknown
    d. "A penny saved is a penny earned." Unknown

8. If this day had also been Alexander's birthday, what present would he have received?
    a. A baseball.
    b. A truck.
    c. Railroad Track Pajamas.
    d. A Mickey Mouse night light.

9. Short essay. Did this book accurately portray the developmental concerns of a seven-year old boy? Give examples to support your ideas.

_____

_____

_____

Key for the <u>Alexander</u> Quiz.

1. b.
2. b.
3. Flunked an exam, overslept and missed a class, sprained his ankle during intramurals, spilled spaghetti all over his new shirt, etc.
4. b.
5. d.
6. d.
7. c.
8. c.
9. Considering Alexander' age and that he is the youngest in the family, his concerns seem pretty typical of this developmental phase. Concern over friends, trying to keep up with older brothers, being a little awkward physically, etc.

Questions 1 and 2 use <u>Recall</u>

Question 3 uses <u>Similarity</u>

Question 4 uses <u>Difference and Similarity</u>

Question 5 uses <u>Cause and Effect</u>

Question 6 uses <u>Example to Idea</u>

Question 7 uses <u>Idea to Example</u>

Question 9 uses <u>Evaluation</u>

Option III - Case Study

This case study offers a situation where students can practice their problem-solving skills. There is no "correct" or even "best" answer and the students face a dilemma that is relevant and realistic.

Students are assigned to small groups of approximately five members. Using a large piece of paper and a magic marker, the students in each groups should discuss the decision-making process using each step of the Problem-Solving Model. After their discussion, they should select a "chosen solution" that the group members believe that Darlene should pursue. When the group has completed their discussion, they will present their process and proposed solution to the other groups. Provide each group with individual copies of the model that follows on the next page.

After the presentations have been given by the groups, take some time to process the different solutions offered by each group. Did every group come up with the same proposed solution? Why or why not? Did groups identify different advantages (positives) or disadvantages (negatives) in their decision-making process?

Problem-Solving Case Study

Darlene Washington is beginning her senior year in college. She is a Communications major and she hopes to enter the field of television when she graduates. She is excited about her senior year because she has been elected the Vice President of her university's student government. During the Spring term of her Junior year, Darlene had an internship at a local television station. This experience only confirmed her decision to pursue a career in the broadcasting field.

One week prior to the fall term, her intern supervisor calls Darlene and offers a starting position at the television station. The starting salary seems fair and this could be such a good opportunity to break into the profession. However, it will mean she will not graduate with the senior class and will have to resign as Vice President of the student government.

What should Darlene do?

Use the Problem-Solving Model in <u>Keys to Success</u> on page 89, to determine a solution to Darlene's dilemma.

Journaling Activities

What was the last really good decision I made? What did I do or consider that made this particular decision work so well? How did I know it was a good decision?

When someone questions or challenges my intellectual abilities what do they say? What do I hear? How do I respond? When was the last time I had this experience? Do I hear failure? Do I hear success?

I experience some fears or phobias when learning about ...
How do I manage my fears?

When was the last major decision that I made but later regretted? Were there any early signals that I did not heed that gave me some clues about the outcome of this decision? Why did I choose not to consider the clues?

When was the last time I reevaluated a position I had on some issue or value? What made me rethink my earlier belief or decision?

Evaluating Student Mastery and Application
Chapter 4

Objective Test Questions

1. Use an analogous or similar thinking pattern to determine the correct answer.
PREFER is to LIKE as SAFE is to
    a. VALUABLE
    b. SECURE
    c. KEEP
    d. DEPEND
    e. WANT

2. Because you have noticed that you get sick whenever you eat a certain food, you have
decided to avoid this food. What type of thinking are you using to make this decision?
    a. Distinction or difference
    b. Prediction or cause and effect
    c. Categorization or idea to concept
    d. Evaluation

3. An essay question for an exam asks you to CONTRAST the two tragic characters,
Hamlet and Willie Loman. You are being asked to focus upon
    a. The similarities between the characters
    b. The strengths of each character
    c. The differences between the characters
    d. The motives of the characters

4. In the following number sequence <u>6</u>, <u>11</u>, <u>16</u>, you determine that the next number that
should follow is <u>21</u>. What thinking activity are you using according to the Thinktrix
Model?
    a. Analysis
    b. Prediction
    c. Valuation
    d. Ranking
    e. Discrimination

5. In a Political Science class you are asked to illustrate how a special interest group
could influence the votes of the Congressional members. What thinking activity is the
professor asking you to demonstrate?
    a. Idea to Example
    b. Example to Idea
    c. Recall
    d. Differences

6. Brainstorming uses which of the following strategies in generating ideas and examples?
    a. Critiques for economic viability
    b. Evaluates for the quality of the idea
    c. Traces the historical significance
    d. Develops the rationale
    e. All of the above
    f. None of the above

7-17. Matching. Match the following concepts with the definition.

___7. Intuition

a. A general point of view or outlook

___8. Perspective

b. An observation of the essential facts or elements.

___9. Thinktrix

c. A determination of the value of something

___10. Description

d. Observation of likenesses between two concepts or objects.

___11. Brainstorm

e. A set of mind actions or types of thinking.

___12. Prediction

f. Knowing something without apparent rationale or evidence

___13. Analogy

g. A method for freely generating innovative ideas

___14. Evaluation

h. A prediction about the future based on the observation of the consequence or pattern

___15. Categorization

I. Substantiation of an idea through information of facts

Essay and Short Answer.

List the steps to problem solving and trace the problem-solving steps using the following as your illustration or example: *where to take someone on the first date.*

_____

_____

_____

Key to Objective Test Questions

1. b.
2. d.
3. c.
4. b.
5. a.
6. f.
7. f.
8. a.
9. e.
10. b.
11. g.
12. h.
13. d.
14. c.
15. i.

References

Browne, M. Neil & Keeley, Stuart M. (1986). *Asking the Right Questions* Englewood Cliffs, N.J.: Prentice-Hall Inc.

Certon, Marvin (1994). *"74 trends that will affect america's future and yours"* The Futurist.

deBono, Edward (1973). *Lateral Thinking.* New York: Harper & Row, Publishers.

Lewis, Hunter (1990). *A Question of Values.* San Francisco, CA.: HarperCollins.

McCarthy, Michael (1991). *Mastering the Information Age.* New York: St. Martins Press.

Miles, Curtis & Rauton, Jane (1987). *Thinking Tools.* Clearwater, FL.: H&H Publishing Company, Inc.

Nist, Sherrie & Diehl, William (1994). *Developing Textbook Thinking.* Lexington, MA.: D. C. Heath and Company.

Prince, George M. (1970). *The Practice of Creativity.* New York: Harper & Row, Publishers, Inc..

vonOech, Roger (1983). *A Whack on the Side of the Head.* New York: Warner Books, Inc..

Word Keys: Communication Through Writing
Chapter 5

Key Concepts: The need for America's citizens to read and write effectively is more critical than ever. In fact, most professional positions will require that individuals spend at least 10% of their working day learning additional skills and new information.

Additional Ideas to Explore with Students. This chapter contains a number of "meaty" concepts in terms of skills for college competencies that are necessary to academic success. Ideas that you may wish to highlight in conjunction with the textbook information is as follows:

Reading

Students' rate of reading should reflect their <u>familiarity</u> with the material, the degree of <u>difficulty</u> of the material and the level of <u>mastery</u> that is required by the class. In general, students resist previewing the material because they believe that it is an unnecessary step. However, cognitive psychologists have noted the multiple benefits to previewing. Previewing allows the brain to establish an organizational structure for the concepts which significantly improves remembering the information. In addition, the preview process cues the students as to the degree of difficulty and the length of time needed to read the material. Also, asking questions while previewing can facilitate curiosity and focus.

Reading to Remember.

Frequently students use a highlighter to identify key concepts in their reading. Unfortunately, there is a tendency for many students to "overhighlight" which essentially results in minimal selectivity and critical analysis. Encouraging students to highlight not more than 10% is a helpful rule of thumb. Making notations while reading can facilitate an organizational structure for reading. (See Option III in the Individual Assignments section)

Taking Notes.

A student needs to determine early in a course what level of notetaking for the class reading will be needed to understand and remember the information.

> *If the material is familiar and the level of mastery needed is general, then notations and highlighting may be adequate.

> *If the material is somewhat familiar and/or the level of mastery is more demanding, then summary sheets akin to the Think Link may be needed.

> *If the material is difficult and/or the level of mastery is extensive, then writing detailed notes, like an outline, may be in order.

Reviewing Alone

The critical times to review class material is within 24 hours of hearing it or reading it, one week after exposure and right before the exam. For optimal results, reviewing strategies should generally be congruent with the student's learning style. So for example, a verbal person will probably benefit significantly from the use of a study group and a more visual learner may benefit more from "pictures" and graphs of the key concepts.

Reviewing With Others

Study groups are very worthwhile for many students. Understanding how to set up a study group will maximize the investment of time for the study group meeting. Generally, study groups should be 3-5 members. Assignments of what is expected from each study session facilitate a more efficient use of the time. It helps to formalize the meeting time and place so all members take the study group time seriously.

Writing College Papers.

College writing places heightened demands upon students. Instead of simply presenting a collection of ideas or information, students now need to consider who their audience will be, how to present a concept to the friendly skeptic, and how to conduct a thoughtful and thorough analysis. In high school, students usually write reports that provide the reader with a general overview of a given topic. But as college students, research writing more often takes the form or analysis and persuasion. A helpful slogan that can communicate the level of maturity and depth needed in their writing is as follows:

"You must do more than simply fertilize the soil,
your writing must now dig for oil."

Individual Assignments

Option I - Reading Speed and Attention Span

This activity is designed to help students become more cognizant of their reading speed and concentration level. Students should select one textbook from one of their courses. They should read ten pages and determine the length of time that it takes to fully comprehend the material on the ten pages. When they have completed the reading activity and timed themselves, they should complete the following "Assessment of My Reading" worksheet.

The determination of one's attention span is based on the number of minutes they can read before his or her mind begins to wander and the number of words that he or she has read. Students should not preview or skim the material prior to reading. They should read three separate times in the same chapter in a quiet and comfortable location. Record keeping and timing should be done and then students should answer the questions about the implications of their current concentration span.

Assessment of My Reading

Textbook Title_____

Beginning Page_____

Ending Page_____

Time lapsed_____

# of pages that the student predicts that he/she could read in one hour____

Next, students will determine their attention span (the number of minutes they can read before their mind begins to wander) and the number of words that are read. Students should not preview or skim prior to commencing their reading. They should just read three separate times for the same chapter in a quiet and comfortable location. Record keeping should be maintained.

1.   How long was the student able to read the first time without breaking their concentration?_____minutes. Their total number of pages read_____.

2.   How long was the student able to read the second time without breaking their concentration?_____minutes. Their total number of pages read_____.

3.   The third time?_____minutes. Their total number of pages read_____.

4.   What are their thoughts about their ability to remain focused in your reading?

_____

_____

_____

5.   Are there any changes or accommodations that the student can make to enhance their focus and concentration?

_____

_____

_____

6.   Were the distractions more likely to be internal (worries, daydreaming,) or external (hallway noise, music, or television)?

_____

_____

Option II - Advance Organization for Reading

Students should quickly preview Chapter 6 in the <u>Keys to Success</u> textbook. Their previewing should be done in five minutes or less. Then students should answer the following questions about the chapter.

How many pages does the chapter have?_____

How long does the student predict that the chapter will take to read and comprehend?
_____

Does the material seem like relatively new material or review information?
_____

_____

_____

What are five key topics that seem to be featured in the chapter?
_____

_____

_____

_____

Write one question about the topic of the chapter.
_____

Are there any study guides or charts that appear helpful?
_____

_____

Option III - Reading to Remember

Using the underlining, highlighting and notation skills discussed in class, demonstrate how you would approach the textbook material in this passage from *Sociology* by John J. Macious. This selection focuses on the observations made by Carol Gilligan about the Gender Factor.

...Gilligan (1982,1990) set out systematically to compare the moral development of females and males. Simply put, her conclusion is that females and males tend to have a different process of moral reasoning. Males, she contends, have a justice perspective, relying on formal rules or appealing to abstract principles to reach judgments about right and wrong. Boys, playing soccer say, are quick to condemn one of their number for touching the ball with his hands or ignoring a boundary line on the field. Girls, on the other hand, have a care and responsibility perspective, which leads them to judge a situation with an eye toward personal relationships and loyalties. Girls playing soccer may be quick to reassure a player who has accidentally touched a ball with her hands. In other situations, breaking a rule may not be perceived as wrong if it is done to help someone else who is in need.

Worth noting is the fact that rule-based male reasoning according to Kohlberg's analysis, is morally superior to person-based female thinking. Gilligan's point is that we must be careful not to set up male standards as the norms by which we evaluate everyone. She reminds us that the impersonal application of rules has long dominated men's lives in the workplace. Concern for attachments, by contrast, has been more relevant to women's lives as wives, mothers, and caregivers. But should we assume that the first approach to moral reasoning is somehow better than the second?

Macionis, John.(1995). *Sociology*.
Englewoods: Prentice-Hall Inc.

Classroom Activities

Option I - Think Link or Mindmap Practice

This activity may be particulary meaningful as a review activity three to five days before an exam in this class. Small groups of students will summarize course material for the other members of the class.

1. Students should be reminded that they should read all of the assigned chapters because they will need to be familiar with the concepts. It would also be beneficial to remind students to bring their textbook and class notes to the class.

2. In dyads or triads students are instructed to develop a Think Link or Mindmap of the key concepts from a specific chapter or class lecture. Each group is instructed to create the Think Link or the Mindmap as a review tool for their classmates. Each group will have 10-15 minutes to create their Think Link/Mindmap from the key concepts.

3. Each group records their Think Link/Mindmap on an overhead transparency using two-three colored marker pens. When the groups have completed their overhead, a representative from the group will present their Think Link/Mindmap to the rest of the class. Other students can ask questions for clarification.

4. It may be desirable to make copies of all of the Think Links and Mindmaps for distribution to the rest of the class during the next meeting.

Option II - Evaluating Persuasive Arguments

Students break into groups of three to five members. Three *fictitious* examples of persuasive statements are distributed to each group to read and review. (See the following page) Student groups should select a recorder to note their reflections and observations.

Groups should use the following questions to guide their discussions.

1. What is the conclusion or argument of the author of the passage?

_____

_____

2. What evidence does the author give for their conclusion?

_____

_____

3. Is there information that is missing or excluded that could alter the conclusion?

_____

_____

4. Is the evidence distorted or unclear?

_____

_____

5. Is there faulty reasoning in the writer's argument? Explain.

_____

_____

6. Does the evidence support the conclusions? Why or why not?

_____

_____

7. What additional information do you need for a better understanding of the issue?

_____

Passage 1

Americans are better off than ever. Twenty years ago, only one in every ten families made over $25,000 and now seven out of every ten families make more than $25,000. Additionally, home ownership has gone up more than 100% in the same period. And finally, the number of personal computers has multiplied five times in the last two decades. These trends clearly indicate that the U.S. is still on top financially in the international marketplace.

Passage 2

A large number of hyperactive children were observed before and after eating food containing large amounts of additives. Before ingesting the additives, 30% of the children exhibited behavior problems; after eating the additives, 60% of the children exhibited problematic behavior. On the basis of this data, it is clear that parents who have hyperactive children should never allow them to eat food with additives.

Passage 3

A United States Congressman sent surveys to his constituencies and found that 75% of the respondents believe that fewer tax dollars should be spent to support our country's National Parks or any endangered species programs. Such an overwhelming response is strong evidence that U.S. taxpayers do not want to fund our nation's park system. The voters have spoken.

Option III - Writing and Editing

Students reflect on what key adjustments they have encountered since beginning their first year at college. What advice would they give to a new student about successfully making the transition to college? Then assign students a one page essay that describes their adjustment to college and their advice to fellow students. Students will have 2-5 days to compose a "discovery draft" of their essay.

On the day that the "discovery draft" is due, students will pair up with another student during class. Their assignment is to critique their partner's "discovery draft". Partners should read one another's paper and make notations for grammar, spelling, organization and content. The students should use the three "C" approach to writing a paper (clarity, conciseness, and concrete development) that is explained on page 112 of the textbook. After the student has written their critique, the partners should verbally share their feedback with one another.

Students should rework their essay based on the feedback that they received and turn it into you for a final grade. Students should submit their "discovery draft", their final draft and the Critique from their partner. Grading will reflect not only their own essay but also the quality and thoughtfulness of the critique they prepare of their peer's essay.

See next page for Critique Form

Critique of Discovery Draft

Name of Writer_____

Name of Editor_____

Comments on Clarity _____

_____

_____

_____

Comments on Conciseness_____

_____

_____

_____

Comments on the Concrete development of ideas_____

_____

_____

What is the thesis statement?_____

_____

Is the thesis well developed?_____

_____

_____

Suggestions for improvements_____

_____

Please make notations for grammar, spelling, organization of the draft itself, using a pen or pencil in a contrasting color.

Journaling Activities

Some topics that are difficult for me to be objective about include....

When I do poorly on an exam, I feel like...

When I do well on an exam, I feel like...

The best ways for me to prepare for an exam are...

Since coming to college, I have discovered that my study skills are...

My high school (community college) prepared me well for academic success by...

I wish that my high school (community college) had prepared me better for college by...

Evaluating Student Mastery and Application

Chapter 5 - Objective Test Questions

1. According to the textbook, there are four general motivations for writing that include informing the reader, creating a literary work, persuading the reader and
    a. Inspiring the reader.
    b. Expressing oneself.
    c. Describing an approach to a problem.
    d. Organizing goals and strategies.

2. The thesis statement for a major paper provides the reader with
    a. A purpose for the paper.
    b. A sense of organization for the paper.
    c. A sense of momentum for the paper.
    d. An agenda for what the paper will attempt to prove.
    e. All of the above.

3. Thinktrix is to the critical thinking processing as Think Link is to
    a. the depiction of key concepts.
    b. the understanding of cause and effect relationships.
    c. the establishment of an experimental design.
    d. the structuring of a series of objectives.

4. What key principles are beneficial to use in successfully writing a college paper?
    a. Write a discovery draft.
    b. Minimize the time between writing the thesis concept and composing the final draft.
    c. Discuss your topic in as broad and general manner as possible.
    d. Keep your writing style as neutral as possible without any special focus on a specific reading audience.

5. To improve reading skills for educational and working content, the student should
    a. Review as soon as possible after reading.
    b. Put concepts in own words.
    c. Think of examples while reading
    d. Reread the preface when reviewing.
    e. All of the above.

6. Previewing should include what components of the textbook content?
   a. Preface
   b. Section headings
   c. Glossary
   d. Table of Contents
   e. Bibliography
   f. All of the above
   g. Two of the above

7. Which strategy is the most effective in generating ideas for a paper?
   a. Write a thesis statement.
   b. Draft an outline.
   c. Compose a discovery draft.
   d. Brainstorm.

Essay and Short Answer.

Knowing Your Audience A Demonstration. Read the following statement regarding federal support for student financial aid. Then rewrite the content in a letter format that is directed to your United States congressman or congresswoman. Keep in mind your audience.

Key ideas to express: The Federal Government should not cut financial aid for university students. If I had to pay more for my education I could not afford to attend college. I already work 20 hours a week and I know that most of my friends are also working part time so they can afford to stay in school.

Dear Congressman/Congresswoman,

_____
_____
_____
_____
_____
_____
_____
_____
_____

What adjustments would you make in your writing if you were expressing your concern about financial aid to a friend? A taxpaying citizen that does not have any children attending college?

_____
_____
_____

Short answer. Evaluate the following proposed thesis statements for a college level research paper on the topic of violence on television. Grade the appropriateness, according to the textbook, of the thesis using a "1" if it strongly meets the characteristics of a good thesis, a "2", if the title is adequate and a "3" if you believe that the thesis is inadequate. In the space provided, write one sentence after each thesis then explains why you evaluated the thesis the way that you did.

Grade (1, 2, 3)

_____ Power Rangers are destroying the moral fabric of our nation.

_____

_____

_____ Television's impact on America's youth can be seen in the increase of violence, the proliferation of guns and the disdain for the Justice System.

_____

_____

_____ Violence in America is a national epidemic and television shares in the responsibility for this dilemma.

_____

_____

_____ "Bang, bang you're dead" is a line too often heard on the television screen and in the streets of America.

_____

_____

Key to Objective Questions

1. b.
2. e.
3. a.
4. a.
5. e.
6. g.
7. d.

References

Goldberg, Natalie (1986). *Writing Down to the Bones*. Boston, MA.: Shambhala
    Publications, Inc..

Kaye, Snadford (1989). *Writing Under Pressure*. New York: Oxford University Press.

Lewis, Jill (1996). *Handbook for Academic Literacy*. Lexington, MA.: D.C. Heath and Company.

Mack, Karin & Skjei, Eric (1979). *Overcoming the Writing Blocks*. Boston, MA.: Houghton
    Mifflin Company.

Roth, Audrey (1989). *The Research Paper*. Belmont, CA.: Wadsworth Publishing Company.

Trimble, John (1975). *Writing with Style*. Englewood Cliffs, N.J.: Prentice-Hall, Inc..

Mind Keys: Retaining What You Learn
Chapter 6

Key Concepts: This chapter is an introduction to various strategies that facilitate enhanced memory and performance on exams. Students are exposed to methods for becoming more intentional in their learning.

Additional Ideas to Introduce to Students: According to cognitive psychologists, the average person forgets 50% of the concepts within twenty-four hours of reading or hearing new information. One week later the amount of information remembered drops to about 35%. For the student, this translates into a need to become more efficient and effective with their study habits. Otherwise, the student will be unprepared for the level of understanding that is required for most college exams. Many students have become accustomed to the last-minute studying that may have resulted in short-term benefits during high school. The proverbial "cramming" session is not adequate to achieve success on college exams.

To stem the tide of forgetting, there are a number of worthwhile learning approaches. In general, adults remember less effectively using rote memory approaches. College students, particularly older adult learners, tend to have more capacity for remembering ideas and concepts if they develop an overview for relating ideas and examples to one another. Seeing the Big Picture seems to facilitate greater mastery of the material. Students can maximize their performance if they reflect upon and review the course concepts throughout the academic term.

Taking class notes that depict the interrelationships between the ideas and the examples is a tool that helps the brain organize the information. While "flash cards" may work well for some students and some subjects, the reviewing of disjointed ideas does not work as well for most students.

Instead, students should use note-taking techniques that express the relationships of the course information and ideas as well as the type of thinking that is needed for the course. For example, a "time line" might be useful in a history class. A chart that shows the similarities or differences between characters could be useful in a Literature class. A mindmap or Thinklink could facilitate learning a theory in Psychology.

Tips for Objective Exams

1. Predict the correct answer to a question before reading the options in a multiple-choice exam.

2. Check the penalties before guessing the answer on objective test questions.

3. Use scratch paper to visualize and problem solve when you are answering questions.

Tips for Essay Exams:

1. Never leave anything blank.

2. Keep the opening paragraph of a longer essay response concise and clear. In general, the opening paragraph should only be two or three sentences in length.

3. Use transition words, like "first," "another" or "next," to keep the paper moving in a well-organized fashion. The transition words alert the instructor that the student is moving to a new idea or example.

4. Remember that the #1 thing that professors look for in a student's essay exam is critical thinking. The ability to articulate an idea or position and then to analyze the cause and effect or development of the idea is a necessary skill for success on essay exams.

5. Leave "white space" at the end of each major essay question response so ideas can be inserted if needed.

6. Write a brief outline or construct a Thinklink prior to composing a response to a major essay question.

7. If a student runs short of time before answering a particular essay question, an outline of the important ideas is a useful alternative to attempting an inadequate, vague answer.

Individual Assignments

Option I - Practicing an Essay Exam

Students generally read their materials over and over prior to an exam but rarely do they actually "practice" taking the exam. Simply reading materials over and over to prepare for an exam is analogous to the cross country athlete who is preparing for a major race by reading a book about running or watching others run around the track. Obviously, the runner prepares for an event by running, sprinting, and working on strength and endurance. In the same way, a good student needs to get ready for an exam by practicing how to take the exam and simulating the same type of thinking that will be required in the exam. So for example, a Literature class will generally stress writing and analysis skills on the exam. On the other hand, an Accounting class usually requires students to solve accounting problems in an efficient and accurate manner.

For this assignment, students must construct one essay question that they predict they might see on their exam in a given class. Students should write the test question and compose a response as if they were actually taking the exam. It is often helpful for students to time themselves while answering the question. This will allow them to experience the same conditions they will have in the exam situation. Often students can find clues about possible test questions from the course syllabus, study guides, and previous exams. In most cases, professors are creatures of habit, and while their actual test questions may change, their format rarely does.

Even if they do not predict one of the actual test questions, the discipline of organizing and expressing their thoughts can help immeasurably in taking the actual exam. A variation on this assignment is to have students create a basic outline or Thinklink of two or three predicted test questions.

Preparing for an Essay Exam

Name of the class_____

Write three possible essay questions that are likely to appear on an upcoming exam.

(a)_____

_____

(b)_____

_____

(c)_____

_____

For one of these questions, write a draft of how you would answer the questions. The essay should be at least 150 words in length.

_____

_____

_____

_____

_____

_____

_____

_____

_____

_____

_____

Option II - Listening Without Talking

This activity requires that students spend an entire meal not talking but just listening to the ideas and feelings of others. The purpose of the exercise is to become more aware of how often individuals in a conversation focus on what they will say next, rather than on what they are hearing from someone else. Students should plan to eat a meal with their family or friends. During the meal, students should not talk and only listen. They should take note of how not engaging in the conversation feels and how often they wanted to engage in the conversation. Did they want to challenge or support the ideas that are being expressed by others?

Shortly after their "listening meal," students should answer the following reflection questions.

1. What were the major topics that were discussed during the meal?

_____
_____
_____

2. When was it most difficult not to say anything and just to listen?

_____
_____

3. Did you see evidence of people not listening to one another or misunderstanding one another? Give examples of times when you noted that others were not really listening or understanding one another.

_____
_____
_____
_____
_____

4. What could people do to listen better to one another?

_____
_____
_____
_____
_____

Option III - Conducting an Exam Evaluation and Critique

Frequently students are eager to get their last exam behind them. Unfortunately, they are missing a valuable opportunity to learn from the exam. What do they now know about their professor and the expectations for the class? What can the students learn about themselves from the exam experience? Yet there is significant learning that can occur after the exam if the student takes the time to reflect on the questions and answers. Also, many faculty post the scores and do not debrief the exam with the students, which only accentuates the tendency to discount the exam results.

Students are to complete the following questionnaire after they have completed an exam. The students may wish to meet with the professor or teaching assistant to gain a better understanding of the content or competencies that are included in the exam.

Course name:_____

How well did you understand the material?_____

_____

_____

Did you make any careless mistakes on the exam?_____

_____

_____

What test-taking strategies did you use preparing and taking this exam?_____

_____

_____

Did you study what the professor considered important for this exam?_____

_____

Were more of the questions drawn from the text or the lecture?_____

_____

Did you allocate your time on the exam well? Explain _____

_____

Did you learn anything in taking this exam?_____

_____

_____

What do you need to do differently in preparing for the next exam?_____

_____

_____

_____

What terms or concepts do you need to (re)learn before moving on in this class? Are there some concepts that you need to understand better?_____

_____

_____

What types of learning or mind actions did you use on this exam? What type of thinking is the professor stressing in this class?_____

_____

_____

Were you surprised by the grade that you received on this exam? Why or why not?

_____

_____

_____

Classroom Activities

Option I - Creating a Mnemonic

Students work in groups of 4-5 members. The group has 5-10 minutes to develop a mnemonic device for remembering the first ten United States presidents in the order of their presidency. They can use an acronym, a jingle, or a sentence that cues them for the ten presidential names. Then one member from each group writes the group's mnemonic device on the board for the other students to view. After each group has presented its mnemonic device, take a few minutes to debrief each device by evaluating its effectiveness.

In general, mnemonics are more successful if they are visual, physically oriented, humorous, or even a little bit absurd. According to Harvard researcher, Robert Ornstein, learning is more likely to occur when the ideas are unique, colorful and dynamic. For example, most individuals cannot remember what they ate for lunch a few days ago but they generally can recall what they ate on a first date with someone they found quite interesting.

Sometimes students create a mnemonic that is as difficult to remember as the original list of concepts. It is helpful to the memory process if the mnemonic has enough of a structure so that it connects back to the original concepts.

Names of the First Ten Presidents:

Washington
Adams, John
Jefferson
Madison
Monroe
Adams, John Quincy
Jackson
Van Buren
Harrison
Polk

Other examples of creating mnemonics might include the first 10-20 chemicals on the Chemical Chart, or other listings of names or disjointed concepts. Mnemonics is a particularly valuable memory tool when students are faced with learning concepts that do not have a clear relationship to one another.

Option II - Writing Exam Questions

This is an excellent way to assist students in preparing for the exam in this class and also illustrating how effective students can be in predicting test questions. Each group of three to five students is responsible for developing seven to ten test questions and writing the questions on five by eight cards. The test questions can be selected from the class lecture material as well as the content of the textbook. It is important to remind students to bring their textbook and their class notes with them to class so the group can peruse through the materials and find potential questions. Students should be instructed to develop questions from at least three major topic areas that have been presented in the class thus far. Questions should include essay, short answer, multiple choice and true-false format types. In addition, the questions should not use only rote memory responses but also deeper thinking approaches. The use of the Thinklink Model can offer students different approaches for thinking about the content.

Before students begin to compile their test questions, each student writes one to two questions individually. Group members share their questions and then the group writes their sample test questions. The groups should write their test questions but not the answers. When they have completed their questions, they should pass along their Question Card to one of the other groups to answer. Each group should respond to the questions written by one of the other groups. When they have finished their answers, the group returns the questions with their responses to the group that originated the questions. The groups then check over the answers for accuracy and clarity.

This process can be repeated so each group develops another list of questions and then answers another list of questions. If there are concerns or clarifications for any of the questions, it is helpful to discuss these with the class as a whole.

*You may choose to make a "Master List" of all of the questions and make it available to students several days prior to the exam and then the exam could feature some or all of the students' sample questions.

Option III - Using Test-Taking Skills

This exercise allows students to discover how good test-taking strategies can facilitate the improvement of their grade. Frequently students take on a "victim" attitude when it comes to taking exams. Seeing how often they can determine correct answers even when they know very little about a topic can be a very significant confidence builder. The questions listed below were taken from a variety of tests in a number of subject areas. In this activity, students are instructed to use every strategy at their disposal to guess the correct answer. More important than the actual correct answer is the resourceful strategies used to figure out the answer. In some cases, the best that they will be able to do is to rule out the incorrect answer. But even that step can be worthwhile during an exam.

Before actually beginning this activity, review some of the tools that are helpful in taking an exam. The following are some of the test-taking approaches that students have at their disposal:

1. Use word prefixes and suffixes to guess the definition of a particular word.

2. Generally, rule out statements with the qualifiers of always, never, all, none, etc.

3. Answer the "easy" questions prior to answering the more "difficult" questions.

4. When numbers are listed for multiple choice options, the middle-range numbers are more likely to be the correct answers.

5. Longer-worded, more comprehensive options in multiple choice questions tend to be true.

6. Sometimes drawing a picture or visualizing the options can help you think through the options and then identify the correct option.

7. Watch for the phrases, "which option is **in**correct" or "which option is **not** true" in the lead sentence of a multiple-choice statement. It is helpful to circle or underline the negative qualifying word so that the correct response can be identified.

8. When there are two similar sounding or similar wordings among the options in a multiple choice question, one of these options tend to be the correct one.

You may want to add other strategies to this list and discuss with the students.

In this activity, each student teams up with one or two other students. The student dyads or triads are instructed to work together to determine which answers on the following test they believe are correct. They should use the test-taking skills as well as common sense to determine which answer they believe is most likely to be correct. The point of this activity is not that they should *know* the correct answer but rather that they use their best hunches and strategies to select the best answer. The students will need to explain what test strategies they have utilized to select their answer or to eliminate the incorrect options.

After the student groups have selected their answers to the Practice Test, then take time as a whole class to report on the answers and share the different strategies that students have utilized. Students hopefully will be able to see that even when taking a test about a subject they do not know about, there are still ways to strategize and at times succeed on exams.

Practice Exam

1. When encoding verbal material into long-term memory, the dominant code used is
   a. Visual
   b. Auditory
   c. Accomplished by considering the meaning of the items
   d. Accomplished by considering the eidetic imagery for the terms

2. Which of the following is a statement of opinion?
   a. The senator is a Republican
   b. Republicans are generally opposed to gun control laws
   c. I can't stand Republicans
   d. All of the above are statements of attitude

3. A monoclinic allotrope is a
   a. Brilliant yellow crystal
   b. Long needle crystal
   c. Brown rubbery solid formation
   d. A red fluid that colors acids

4. What does not belong with the others?
   a. Right pleural cavity
   b. Left pleural cavity
   c. Vertebral cavity
   d. Pericardical cavity

5. In a skeletal twitch, which of the following requires the least amount of time?
   a. Relaxation
   b. Latent
   c. Contraction
   d. Extension

6. A statistical scale of measurement that is used to evaluate the rank order of people is known as a
   a. Nominal scale
   b. Interval scale
   c. Ordinal scale
   d. Ratio scale

7. The "Great Pyramid" originally stood how many feet above sea level?
   a. 81
   b. 381
   c. 481
   d. 1231

8. Which one of the following statements does not illustrate a self-serving bias?
   a. I got an "A" because I am smarter than anyone else in the class
   b. I got fired because the boss didn't like me
   c. I failed the test because the teacher doesn't really know how to teach
   d. I weigh 150 pounds

9. A student showing a pattern of withdrawing from his/her most difficult course each term when the pressure starts to mount and he/she is not doing well is an example of what psychological concept?
   a. Negative reinforcement
   b. Delayed positive reinforcement
   c. Punishment being informative
   d. Cruel and unusual punishment

10. If a church is one of your reference groups
   a. You will evaluate your beliefs and behavior in comparison with other members of the church
   b. Your behavior will be regulated by the members' use of of social reward and punishment
   c. The church group will influence your interpretation of events and social issues
   d. All of the above

Key to Practice Test and Suggestions for Exam Strategies

1. c. Visual and auditory are external physical processes and not related to long-term memory. c. and d. are similar sounding and this may tip student that one of these options should be considered.

2. c. The statements a. and b. are factual and could be proven, and therefore are not a personal point of view or attitude. d. is ruled out because at least one of the previous statements is not an attitude.

3. b. Use the prefix "mono" which means single or alone or the suffix "trope" which means a combining form. If students cannot remember what mono means, they can think of other words that start with prefix "mono" like monolith or monopoly

4. c. Rule out left and right pleural because it is highly unlikely that one can be false and not the other since they are essentially the same thing on different sides of the body. If students use the pleura prefix, they can determine that these terms relate to the lungs and then cardical relates to the heart. Students might recall terms like cardiac arrest to help them figure this out. Since the heart and lungs are in the same general space of the body, it could be assumed that these are the three that belong together.

5. c. In this question, it might be helpful to actually imagine an arm in different physical positions. One could visualize how long it is takes to relax or extend an arm and also how quickly an arm contracts if it comes in contact with if a very hot objective.

6. c. The prefix "ord" appears in both the question and the correct response. Both words indicate an ordering of people by some characteristic.

7. b. Eliminate a. and d. because they are both more extreme heights. Mid-range numbers are more likely to be the correct answer.

8. d. It is important that the student highlight or circle the word "not" to keep that focus in mind. All of the statements, a. b. and c., serve to put the person in a good light and therefore are self-serving. It is very hard to prove the validity of a., b., and c. because these statements illustrate an opinion.

9. a. The d. response uses legal terminology and this is a question from a psychological perspective. There is no indication of positive reinforcement in past, present, or future which makes the b. option less likely.

10. d. Use the term "reference" as the key word or "refer" as the prefix in this question. If someone refers to someone else, then that person has some significance or influence. The statements a., b. and c. all address some type of influence or shaping of the church on an individual. Once a student determines that two of the potential answers is correct, then it is likely that the "all of the above" selection is true.

Option IV - A Listening Exercise

Students often believe that listening is a very basic skill that does not deserve much effort or attention. In fact, the act of active listening is very demanding and even exhausting. A student who is really listening to a lecture for an hour or two should feel some fatigue from focusing on the content. In addition, this activity will illustrate how much erosion occurs in remembering information within 24-48 hours. On Day One, students experience a typical session of this class. No announcement about the next class session should be made during the lecture on Day One.

Within 24-48 hours, at the next class session, a short quiz is given over the concepts that were covered during Day One's class. After students have answered the 5-10 test questions on Day Two, the correct responses are presented and discussed. Then the number of correct answers answered by each student is graphed in a class summary of how well the students performed on the test. The graph will provide a persuasive testimony of the need to review course material in an ongoing fashion. Take time to discuss the test results and what the implications they may have for the necessity of using certain study strategies.

Journaling Activities

What does educational success mean to me?

What does educational failure mean to me?

What do I do that threatens my academic success?

One time when I became so engaged with my learning that I lost all track of time....

I feel most competent as a student when...

Evaluating Student Mastery and Application
Chapter 6

Objective Test Questions

1. An essay exam question that asks a student to COMPARE concepts or characters is expecting the answer to
    a. Point to the similarities between two ideas, characters or approaches.
    b. Briefly develop the history of how something developed.
    c. Express the definition of a word, concept or thing.
    d. Discuss the various components of a larger concept or idea.

2. When approaching a mathematics problem it is not advisable to
    a. First guess what the answer might be approximately.
    b. Work through the problem from the answer backwards if you are stumped.
    c. Check through your answer using logical analysis.
    d. Ask for help from others if you get stuck.
    e. Go with your first computation.

3. When preparing for an exam it is advisable to
    a. Ask the instructor what the focus will be.
    b. Predict possible test questions.
    c. Write out or diagram the key ideas.
    d. Orally recite the important concepts.
    e. All of the above.

4. Which of the following is not an example of a mnemonic device?
    a. Every Good Boy Does Fine associates with the notes on the musical scale.
    b. "Thirty days has September, April, June and November..." aids remembering the number of days in a month.
    c. ROY G BIV helps a student remember the colors of the rainbow.
    d. A time line to remember the historical events.

5. Generally individuals remember concepts if they are grouped into not more than how many ideas or terms?
    a. Five
    b. Ten
    c. Twenty
    d. Twenty-five

6. For which type of exam would flash cards be generally the most helpful in remembering key course concepts?
    a. An Ethics exam
    b. An introductory course in a Foreign Language
    c. A Poetry Literature class
    d. A Macroeconomics course

7. What test strategies while taking an exam are not recommended by the authors of the textbook?
    a. Preview the exam before answering the questions.
    b. Answer the difficult questions first while you are fresh.
    c. Be wary of questions that contain the qualifiers always, never, all or none.
    d. Outline or Thinklink your essay question before writing out the answer.

8. An essay question that asks the student to TRACE a concept or idea is directing the student to
    a. Explain in detail the causes of a particular event.
    b. Make a critical judgment concerning the quality of something.
    c. Historically highlight the events.
    d. Give a definition of a concept.

Short answer and essay questions.

Definitions. Define and give an example or illustration of the following concepts.

Mnemonic_____

Illustration or Example_____

Association (a memory technique)_____

Illustration or Example_____

Essay Question.
List at least three steps a student should take when beginning an exam that can maximize academic performance.

_____
_____
_____
_____
_____
_____

Key to the Objective Test Questions.

1. a.
2. e.
3. e.
4. d.
5. b.
6. b.
7. b.
8. c.

References

Buzan, Tony (1974). *Use Both Sides of Your Brain*. New York: E.P. Dutton.

Buzan,Tony (1984). *Use Your Perfect Memory*. New York: E.P. Dutton

De Porter, Bobbi & Hernacki, Mike (1992) *Quantum Learning*. New York: Dell Publishing Company Inc..

Ostrander, Shelia (1979). *Super Learning*. New York: Dell Publishing Company Inc...

Silver, Theodore (1992). *Study Smart*. New York: Villard Books.

Maintaining the Essentials: Taking Care of Yourself
Chapter 7

Key Concepts: This chapter offers an overview of the health issues and lifestyle choices that are most prevalent among young adults. Students are introduced to the interrelationship of their intellectual acuity, physical well-being and emotional state.

Additional Concepts to Explore with Students: Initially students are somewhat skeptical about the need to understand their physical well-being. In part, this attitude may be attributable to the fact that the vast majority of students have experienced relatively good health up until this time in their lives. Students characteristically have a feeling of invincibility. For some students, discussions about health issues are reminiscent of the reprimands and reminders that they heard from their parents. Phrases like "Eat plenty of vegetables" or "Get eight hours of sleep" are generally not appreciated by young adults that are staking out their independence.

In approaching the subject of health and personal well being, it may be beneficial to use guest speakers to present concepts like nutrition, exercise, and drugs and alcohol. This information will be more openly received by students if there is a clear rationale for the recommendations made concerning healthy lifestyle choices. Students need to know the consequences and effects of the health choices that they make. In addition, there is a wide variety of health concerns between the members of the class. Dependent upon age, lifestyle choices, ethnicity and culture and physical make-up, students are likely to relate very differently to the health issues that are included in this chapter. Therefore, it may be more meaningful to the students if they are encouraged to do additional reading and exploration in the topic area that has the most relevance for them.

One particular topic that is generally a concern for college students is Stress Management. Therefore, it is worthwhile to explore in depth the topic of Stress and Change because this issue is relatively universal with college students. For most students, and for that matter, most adults in America, change is a daily reality. The pace of change is probably only going to accelerate in the next century, so the ability to cope and to even welcome change is a valuable life skill.

Managing Stress

The following is a summary of key concepts that could be presented and discussed during a class session. You may also consider making copies of this material and distributing to the students.

Change and Stress

Change is a fact of life. Nothing remains the same forever. You can't stop the world because you want to get off. Life just keeps rolling along.

But be forewarned. While change can stimulate and stretch you, it may also be hazardous to your health. The stress of adjusting too much in too short of a time period can even make you sick. Research studies have examined the relationships between children who are experiencing a significant number of changes and their accident rates, adults' life change clusters and the onset of illness, and life change clusters and the number of heart attacks. Each study indicates that illness and accidents are more likely to occur as the number of life changes increases.

Additional Observations:

*Positive as well as negative changes contribute to illness.

*The effects of change accumulate over time.

*Major life changes often come in bunches such as marriage, starting college, a death in the family, etc.

*Too little change can also cause illness.

*Each person has different inner signals that alerts him or her to the level of change they experience. Too often humans either don't notice these signals or choose not to understand the meaning of these signals.

*There is a fine line between stress as a tonic and stress that is toxic.

It's hard to control the rate of change in today's hectic world. It's not easy to know what is the most effective pace to maintain. Whether you are going too slowly, rushing too quickly, or experiencing a crisis and feeling out of control, you need to make intelligent decisions about the pace that works well for you. Each person has a unique optimal pace that works well for him or her. Additionally, there are times when each person may vary in his or her most optimal pace. For example, new parents often need to significantly slow down after the birth or adoption of a new child. Bonding and child care takes extra energy from the new parents and may greatly impact how many other activities and responsibilities they can assume.

Making Choices About Stress and Change

1. Learn the ways that your body, mind, and emotions signal you when you are experiencing a toxic level of stress. Some individuals experience migraine headaches, others have a backache or even a cold that just does not seem to go away. Also, sleeping more or less than usual may be a signal of some over-stress. Even an emotional state may offer a signal of your stress level. Can you recognize your stress symptoms?

2. Learn how and when to say "No". There are times when it is essential to decline any additional commitments. Saying "yes" when you are already over committed often leads to disappointing results and a disabling sense of stress.

3. Plan your changes carefully. Postpone changes that are optional if there are already too many unavoidable changes. Very often each major change is accompanied by many smaller changes. For example, when one marries they not only are learning to live with someone else but they are also getting acquainted with the spouse's family and friends.

4. Avoid impulsive changes. Carefully weigh out the positive and negative effects of each decision. Anticipate problems and negative consequences and try to head them off in advance.

5. Once you make a change, move ahead boldly. Act with courage and don't constantly look back wondering what might have been. Make certain to ask for the help and support of those who are close to you so you do not have to make each step of the change alone.

6. Relax and practice becoming more flexible. Give yourself the freedom to do some things less than perfectly. Learn how to roll with the punches and when to laugh at yourself a little. The adaptable people are more likely to make it through periods of stress without falling apart. Don't worry about every little venture that did not go as you had planned.

7. Learn how to take care of yourself. Generally, you will be able to cope with more change if you are in good emotional and physical condition. Invest in your well being. When you are experiencing additional stress in your life, nurture yourself with some activity that brings special pleasure to you.

Individual Assignments

Option I - Making Meaning

Physical and mental well-being is significantly impacted by the manner in which different individuals perceive their life experiences and encounters. College students are generally at a point in their life when they can reevaluate their lifestyle and values because they are in transition and are establishing their own values and traditions apart from family influence. The following activity attempts to assist students in understanding their beliefs and expectations. In large part, the stress that individuals experience comes from the meaning that is individually attributed to experiences and encounters.

Psychologists such as Albert Ellis have suggested that the meaning an individual derives from a particular circumstance may in fact be more influential than the actual circumstance. In other words, the meaning that one derives from an event is what influences the subsequent attitude and behavior of that individual. In much more eloquent language, this concept is echoed by Viktor Frank in his book <u>Man's Search for Meaning</u>. It is from the personal meaning that an individual determines how he or she will respond.

In a brief summary, this concept is depicted in the following model. By viewing the model with a relevant experience, it becomes clearer how this model could be applied to the lives of students.

The model is followed by a specific illustration, so students can explore the model using two different situations. Then the students explore some of their own beliefs and how those beliefs may influence their attitudes, behavior, and stress level.

Activating Event------------Meaning------------Consequences

Activating Event is a <u>Breakup With A Significant Other</u>.

The Meanings or Beliefs that different individuals ascribe to this activating event could include:

*I've lost the man/woman of my dreams; there will never be another person like him/her.

*All men/women are alike. You just can't trust them.

*Maybe I need more time to find out who I am and get my career started.

*There will be another person in the future who will be even better for me.

The consequences of these various meanings could be very different. For the person who believes that all men are alike and can't be trusted, it is likely that her behavior following the breakup would demonstrate a general skepticism about men/women or instead she/he could end up going out with a man/woman who is untrustworthy because his behavior would likely only confirm her beliefs. Or, if someone believes that there will be someone else down the road, there is a positive attitude toward future dating even if there is an initial sense of loss or sadness.

Making Meaning

Activating Event #1: Failing a class in Anatomy and Physiology

1. What different meanings might someone make from this event?

a._____

_____

b._____

_____

c._____

_____

d._____

_____

e._____

_____

2. Based on these various meanings, what different ways could individuals behave or feel after this event?

a._____

b._____

c._____

d._____

e._____

Activating Event # 2 : Due to limited budget you are unable to fly home for Thanksgiving.

1. What different meanings might someone make from this event?

a._____

b._____

_____

c._____

_____

d._____

_____

e._____

_____

2. Based on these various meanings, what different ways could individuals behave or feel after this activating event?

a._____

b._____

c._____

d._____

e._____

Now think about some activating event in your own life and walk through the same steps. Examples of some events you might include are any of the following: unable to decide on my major; not getting along with my roommate; gaining some weight since starting school; parents selling the family home that I grew up in as a child.

My activating event is _____

The meaning that I have created from this event is

_____

_____

_____

_____

My current behavior and feelings about the event_____

_____

_____

_____

_____

_____

Some ways that I might adjust my meaning about this event in a more constructive manner might be

_____

_____

_____

Ways that I could adjust or change my current attitude and behavior include

_____

_____

_____

_____

_____

Option II - Making a New Health Habit

In this assignment students have the opportunity to explore the challenge of changing or enhancing a personal health habit. Students select one health habit in their life that they believe could use some change. This habit could relate to sleeping patterns, eating choices, exercise program, or any other physical concerns. For one week, they should determine one small but significant change that they could make in the health habit and how they would make a change. The goals should be specific, reasonable and measurable. For example the goal, "I want to get more sleep" is too general and is difficult to measure. However, the goal of "I want to get to sleep by midnight every night this week" is specific and measurable.

During an entire week, students track their progress (or lack of progress) in achieving their new habit. Students should maintain a journal that briefly comments on how well the new habit is becoming incorporated daily. Then at the end of the week, students respond to the following self-observation questions.

Self-Observation on Changing a Habit

According to your journal, how successful were you in achieving your goal?

_____

_____

_____

_____

Did you set a goal that was too easy or too difficult to achieve?

_____

_____

Were there certain people, circumstances, or locations that undermined your motivation to stick to your goal?

_____

_____

_____

What people, circumstances, or locations supported your motivation to achieve your goal?

_____

_____

Did you have some group or person to whom to be accountable for sticking with your goal?

_____

_____

What would you do differently if you were to set the same goal for next week? Would you alter your goal statement at all? If yes, how would you rework it?

_____

_____

_____

Option III - A Picture of My Stresses

Consider what factors in your life are contributing to your stress level. Some of these stressors may actually be positive, others may be negative and some might have both negative and positive effects for you. Picture or write those stressors that are negative on the left-hand side of the paper and those things that are positive on the right-hand side of the paper. Those things that are both negative and positive should be placed in the middle section of the paper. For example, your new job might be positive because you really like the people you are working with, but the hours you work may create some negative stress. When you have finished your Picture of Stress, then answer the questions at the bottom of the page.

Are there any stressors that you can eliminate?_____

_____

Is your level of current stress toxic or tonic to you?_____

_____

What support do you need? What changes can you make to cope with your stressors?

_____

_____

_____

Classroom Activities

Option I - Role Playing Scenarios

In this activity students practice communication skills that can be used in confronting a student who is making unhealthy choices. Students in the class are divided into groups of 3-5 each. A scenario is given to each group to discuss and then to dramatize for the rest of the class. Groups should offer an approach for constructively and positively dealing with the situation in the scenario they receive. Groups are to "cast" their group members into whatever roles they want to act out their assigned scenario. Their objective is to develop a skit that enacts the situation and a reasonable manner for confronting the dilemmas. After each skit is presented, there is a debriefing with the entire class on the resolution dramatized as well as other alternatives or considerations.

Scenario I - Drinking Roommate

Your roommate has come in very late three nights out of the last week. It isn't just the lateness that concerns you, but the excessive alcohol consumption. You have not seen him study in weeks. Additionally, you have noticed that because he is hung over so often, he rarely makes it to any of his morning classes.

You really like your roommate and when you first started living together, you seemed to have a lot in common. At this point, you are not very close but you would like to remain roommates. Since his girlfriend from his hometown broke up with him, he seems to be unmotivated and even a little depressed. You believe that if your roommate does not get a handle on his drinking, he is going to flunk out of college.

What do you do? Whom do you talk to? What do you say to your roommate?

Scenario II - Bulimic Team Member

You are a new member of the Gymnastics team on campus and you are very excited about the potential for the team to win the championship this year. The women on the team are very talented and very competitive. At the same time, the team members are very supportive of one another. The work-outs and the training are very demanding but it all seems to be worth the effort.

Prior to one of the meets, you notice that the captain of the squad eats a very big meal and then scarfs down a whole box of Oreo cookies. A half-hour after she has eaten, you find her in the bathroom throwing up. You ask her if she is alright and she laughs and tells you that she just feels a little nauseated - too much food and too many jitters before the meet. You decide that she is probably right and that she is just a little stressed out.

A week later at a major competition out of state, you are rooming with the captain. You find wrappers of a dozen candy bars in the waste paper basket. Later that night you find your roommate hanging over the toilet and throwing up again. Now you suspect that the problem is not just a case of nerves but some type of eating disorder.

What do you do? Whom do you talk to? What do you say to her?

Scenario III - Too Many Commitments

You are a newly elected senator for the student government. One of your best friends urged you to run so you could be involved in the student senate together. This friend is someone you really admire so you were very flattered by her encouragement.

Your friend seems to "do it all." She is an honors student with a double major, works 20-30 hours a week, and maintains an active leadership role in the student government, the Psychology Club, the Choir, and also tutors children at a local school. Whenever a job needs to be done, your friend volunteers.

Somehow your friend is able to maintain this incredible pace for weeks on end until she gets so run down that she gets quite sick. Her illness lasts a few days and then she is back at her break-neck pace. You are concerned that the next time she gets sick, it will even be more serious.

What do you do? Whom do you talk to? What do you say to your friend?

Option II - Case Studies

The subject of sexual harassment and date rape is one that is very difficult for many to discuss, especially men and women together. By offering a couple of case studies for discussion, students may be in a better position to understand some of the issues and also how to communicate more openly with one another. You may want to discuss these case studies as a whole class or divide the class into smaller sub-groups.

Before beginning, it may be helpful to discuss some criteria for evaluating these delicate issues.

Case Study I - Study Group

Jessica and Kyle have been in the same science class for over six weeks. They are also members of a class study group that has largely been successful due to Kyle's obvious knowledge about the subject area. Jessica is grateful to Kyle for his willingness to help the members of the study group sessions. In fact, Kyle has been willing to tutor Jessica for a short time after the study group. Academic success in this class may make the difference for Jessica's acceptance into Nursing School, a dream she has had since she was a little girl.

One evening after the study group has finished meeting, Jessica asks Kyle a few specific questions that she has about the material. Kyle approaches Jessica for a date. While the idea is not totally a surprise to Jessica, she sees Kyle as only a friend and doesn't want to send mixed signals. When she tells Kyle that she does not feel that dating is a good idea, Kyle becomes very frustrated and tells her that he does not see the study group as worth his time if he does not have an opportunity to get to know her better. Jessica knows that the rest of the study group will be very disappointed if Kyle leaves the group.

Is Jessica being sexually harassed?

Is this a fair expectation for Kyle to have?

How should Jessica handle this situation?

Should the rest of the group be involved?

Case Study II - Engineering Class

Teresa is the only female in an engineering class filled with all males. The professor is a male in his mid-fifties who is a good teacher but very traditional in his opinion of women. In the beginning of the class, the professor made some light, teasing comments about how nice it was to have a "pretty face" in the class. He has also complimented Teressa about what she was wearing in front of the other students. While the other students have not joined in with the teasing, it is obvious that the male students think that the professor's comments are funny and all in good fun. Teresa does not want to appear to be thin-skinned so she has usually laughed the comments off or said nothing.

In the last few weeks, Teresa has noticed that the teasing comments are getting a little more sexual in nature. Comments like "You probably do not have trouble getting study help from the other students with the perfume you are wearing" or "I sure wish there were more good looking women in engineering classes when I was a student" are beginning to make Teresa feel very discounted as a serious student and very anxious as a woman.

Is this an example of sexual harassment?

Is the professor just trying to be funny?

How should the female student handle this situation?

Should others be involved in this response? How and who?

What if the professor offered to tutor this female student at his home?

Option III - Understanding Disabilities

Many students are relatively uncomfortable and unfamiliar with challenges that students with disabilities face. This class activity offers the class an excellent opportunity to understand better the physical, social and academic challenges that students with disabilities encounter daily. It may also be helpful for some students who suspect that they have a disability such as a learning disability and are uncertain how to get support and accommodations. Contact the university's Office for Students with Disabilities for assistance.

One approach to this class exploration is to schedule a panel of students with disabilities and/or the professional staff that serve the disabled students. This panel could share how disabilities impact the personal and academic spheres of students' lives. Be sure to offer the opportunity for the class to ask questions realizing that there may be some reticence initially. If students appear to be a little cautious, then soliciting questions anonymously on cards may help them respond.

A second approach is to have students actually experience a disability for a period of time. Students can use wheelchairs or crutches, wear glasses that limit their vision, or listen to a tape of a textbook instead of reading it. This simulation experience should last at least 30-60 minutes so there can be a sense of the actual discomfort and difficulty of the experience. The Office of Disabilities may be able to assist you in coordinating this project. After the experience, have a class discussion about their personal feelings and also their observations about what areas on the campus are not very supportive of students with disabilities.

Journaling Activities

What health habits and personal priorities help me feel best about my physical health and appearance ?

Since beginning college, what am I doing to enhance my physical well-being? What am I doing that may be undermining my physical health?

As I look at my current energy level I am noticing ......

I could reenergize myself by doing more/less of.......

Evaluating Student Mastery and Application
Chapter 7

Objective Test Questions

1. Which of the following is not one of the three major categories of exercise described in the textbook?
    a. Latent stress training
    b. Cardiovascular training
    c. Strength training
    d. Flexibility training

2. What percentage of Americans will experience a major depression during their lifetime?
    a. Less than 5%
    b. Approximately 10%
    c. Close to 25%
    d. Over 35%

3. Physical dependence is most likely to occur with which of the following types of drugs?
    a. Depressants
    b. Inhalants
    c. Hallucinogens
    d. Stimulants
    e. a. and d.
    f. a. and c.

4. Codeine is an example of what category of drugs?
    a. Depressants
    b. Cannabinols
    c. Hallucinogens
    d. Opiates
    e. Stimulants

5. According to reported percentages, which of the following is the most effective form of birth control?
    a. Depo-Provera
    b. Intra-uterine device
    c. Diaphragm
    d. Condom

6. Which statement about stress is not true?
    a. Stress is caused by change in one's life
    b. Stress is negative and should be avoided
    c. Stress can contribute to physical illness
    d. People vary widely in the amount of stress they can manage effectively

7. An enabler is someone who
    a. Introduces others to new ideas
    b. Becomes overly invested and involved in supporting an addict
    c. Keeps communication open and honest
    d. Capitalizes on personal strengths

8. Exercise contributes to one's well being in which of the following ways?
    a. Helps individual cope with heightened stress levels
    b. Maintains personal flexibility and strength
    c. Facilitates cardio-vascular strength for an individual
    d. Enhances quality of sleep for person
    e. All of the above

Essay and Short Answer Questions

Discuss how to establish a program for changing a health habit using the principles discussed in this class. Use a hypothetical health habit to illustrate your points.

_____
_____
_____
_____
_____

Essay. List five signals that could indicate that someone has an alcohol drinking problem.

_____
_____
_____
_____
_____

Key for Objective Test Questions

1. a.
2. b.
3. e.
4. d
5. a.
6. b.
7. b.
8. e.

References

Bridges, William (1980). *Transitions*. Reading, MA.: Addison-Wesley Publishing Company.

Edlin, Gordon & Golarty, (1982). *Health and Wellness*. Boston, MA.: Science Books International.

Vickery, Donald and Fries, James (1994). *TakeCare of Yourself*. Reading, MA: Addison-Wesley Publishing Company.

Films and Videos for Class Use.

Fit or Fat for the Nineties
   Distributed by PBS, 1320 Baddock Place, Alexandria, VA 22314
   A 77-minute video providing current research and data on diet, exercise and health habits in an entertaining, informative manner.

Wellness
   (1989), Distributed by Great Performance Inc., 700 N. Green St. Suite 302, Chicago, Illinois 60622

Personal Power: Assuring Progress
Chapter 8

Key Concepts: This chapter continues the process of self-exploration that earlier chapters introduced. Now students look at the values that fuel their goals and their motivation to achieve those goals. The issue of how to deal with success and failure constructively is also addressed.

Additional Concepts to Explore: Some students (and perhaps even instructors) might wonder about why the topics of ethics, integrity, and values are featured in a class on college success. Yet these issues are critical to the sense of empowerment and personal direction that most students need to define as they establish themselves as independent and interdependent adults.

The annual research conducted by Alexander Astin with college freshman over the last twenty-five years indicates a growing value among students for focusing on only what impacts them in a personal way. Earning more money, taking care of their own family, and engaging in a profession that assures them success have taken over as the priorities that have taken over for this generation of students. Most students are not too confident with America's institutions because they have observed that most, if not all, of these institutions are flawed and failing. It seems that making commitments is very difficult for young adults today because they are uncertain about what awaits them in the future. Their response has recently been to "keep their options open" so they do not have to be committed to anything that ultimately may disappoint them.

The next pages provide a summary of some of these trends and also some provocative quotes that might be worthy of class discussion.

Trends in College Students' Beliefs and Values

*Prefer style over substance.

*Want information on demand, in bite-size pieces, with many choices.

*Postpone major life commitments and settling down.

*Believe that people pay for results .

*Want to spend more time with their children than their parents spent with them.

*Believe that a two-income family is the reality of the future.

*See the faster pace and competition as generally a good thing.

*Feel skeptical about the future of America.

*Tend to be pragmatic and ambitious.

Quotes from Generation X

"The world seems to be falling apart."

(Levine, 1993)

"Ain't nobody lookin' out for me, but me."

(Rap Group)

"Particle man values the physical, muscle matters, style counts, speed is crucial."

(Howe and Strause, 13th Generation)

"If they can't say it an hour, they ought to put it on tape."

(13 year old on going to church)

"The strongest appeal you can make is emotionally. If you can get their emotions going, forget their logic, you've got' em."

(MTV Executive)

Individual Assignments

Option I - A Biography of a Leader

Students today have very few role models to learn from and to emulate. The media creates instant heroes and then destroys them even more quickly. Many adults in leadership or authority positions have disappointed students in the past. This phenomenon is presented in a compelling article entitled "The Making of a Generation" by Arthur Levine. In this article, Levine quotes a student expressing, "Our experience is of flaws, problems, decline. We're not number one in anything. Our generation grew up with that." (Levine, 1993, p. 14)

This has created a situation that has left a significant number of students with a sense of drifting. Many students question the value of institutions and the integrity of individuals. Making commitments and establishing a sense of direction seem to be particularly difficult for this generation of students.

The purpose of this assignment is to facilitate an understanding of the commitments and courage of a great leader. Students are to read a biography of their choice. Some recommendations for a possible biography include the following:

Ashe, Arthur & Rampersad, Arnold (1993). *Days of Grace*. New York: Ballantine Books.

Cook, Blanche (1992). *Eleanor Roosevelt*. New York: Penguin Books.

Delaney, Sarah & Delaney, Elizabeth (1993). *Having Our Say*. New York: Dell Publishing.

Gardner, Howard (1994). *Creating Minds*. New York: Basic Books.

Goldman, Roger & Galler, David (1992). *Justice for All -Thurgood Marshall*. New York:Carol and Graf Publishers, Inc..

Malcolm X (1964). *The Autobiography of Malcolm X*. New York: Ballantine Books.

Mandela, Nelson (1994). *Long Walk toFreedom*. Boston: Little, Brown and Company.

Mead, Margaret (1972). *Blackberry Winter*. New York: Kodarsha International.

Rodruigez, Richard (1982). *The Education of Richard Rodriguez*. New York: Bantam Books.

When students have read the autobiography, they should write a 2-3 page paper that answers key questions about the leader. The paper should summarize the leader's values, goals and motivation. Some possible questions for consideration are offered.

How did the leader provide leadership?

How did the leader manage success and failure?

What values and ethical principles did this leader live by? Were there times of compromise in terms of high standards and ethics?

What motivated this leader?

What were the leader's goals?

How did the leader gain skills in leadership?

What can you learn from the life of this leader?

Option II - An Interview with a Leader

Students are to select a leader who they respect and admire. The "leader" may be a teacher, minister or rabbi, current or former employer, a family friend or relative, or anyone else who has demonstrated leadership. The person whom the students select could be someone they know well or someone they do not know very well at all. However, the person they select needs to be someone who is accessible and that they can interview during the next two to three weeks. The interview could be accomplished over the phone if that is the only option available.

Students should come to the interview prepared with a number of specific questions that will give focus to the time together. After the interview has been conducted, students write a summary of what they learned from their selected leader. The paper should be two to three pages and should not simply be a collection of quotes from the leader. The following is a suggested list of questions that may be helpful to the students.

Some suggested questions that students may select to use in their interview.

1. What is your philosophy of leadership?

2. What basic principles and values do you attempt to live by day by day?

3. Have you experienced a significant failure or setback? How did you attempt to deal with this experience?

4. How do you attempt to refuel themselves?

5. How do you try to motivate others?

6. How do you want to be remembered by others?

7. What advice do you have for your future?

Option III - A Letter to Someone Who Has Made a Difference

For many students, the ability to reflect objectively upon their life and the people who have been influential can be a valuable, maturing experience. It is often through relationships with a few significant people that students' lives have been shaped. Frequently, the students' current commitments to a professional goal and to the pursuit of higher education have been fueled by those significant people.

In this writing assignment, students will actually compose (and hopefully also mail) a letter to someone who has made a difference in their life. This person may have taught the student some valuable life lessons, helped the student through a rough time, modeled excellence or just believed in the student. There may be many ways that the person actually supported the student that can be reflected in the letter.

In this assignment, students are to type a one- to two-page letter to someone who has had a positive impact on their life. The letter should explain how the person made a difference in the life of the student and should include specific examples or stories. Also, the letter should tell the person what the student is currently doing and how the student is still influenced by this significant person.

After the letter has been completed and graded, encourage the students to mail the letters to the significant person. Students may be quite surprised at how much this affirmation means to the person who receives it.

Classroom Activities

Option I - Sharing an Artifact

This activity is a meaningful way for students to reflect more deeply about what is important to them and also a thoughtful way for the classmates to get to know one another. Students are asked to bring two to three artifacts which say something about their personality, their personal history, and what is important to them. Pictures, a special book, a memento of a special event or a gift from someone might be examples of the types of artifacts which students choose to bring to the class. The actual choice for what to bring is up to each student. Whatever they bring will be shown and briefly explained to the rest of the class.

It is probably helpful to give students three to five days to determine what they want to bring as their artifacts. During a class period, the students will show their artifacts to the rest of the class and also explain the significance of the artifacts which they have selected to bring. You may need to give a time limit so students do not get carried away in explaining the meaning of their artifacts. If the class is particularly large you may need to break the class into small groups of 6-8 students. Should you decide to do the smaller groups, you will not have the opportunity to hear what the students share so you might want to have them briefly write on a small card what they brought and why. This will allow you to learn a little more about your students.

Option II - The Story of Jane and John

Listening openly and accurately is always a challenge. But this challenge is even more difficult when two people come at a situation with very different values. This activity is a persuasive illustration of how listening becomes influenced by the different points of view. The first step to this activity is to have all of the students read the story about Jane and John which follows. Then the students will rank the characters in the story according to their estimation of right and wrong.

The Story of Jane and John

Jane and John lived in a town that was divided by a river. They were in love. One night, a tornado swept through the town, tearing down the bridges and knocking out the telephones and electricity. That night, Jane and John were on opposite sides of the river.

Jane was frantic to find John and to determine that he was all right. She went down to the river and met James, who had a boat. However, James had a price for taking Jane across: she would have to have sex with him.

Unwilling to pay the price, Jane went to Wilbur, a rich man in the town who had a helicopter which could take her across. Wilbur told her that she should just wait a few days, because John was most likely O.K..

But Jane was still anxious about John, so she went back to James and paid his price. John was overjoyed to see her. He asked her how she got across the river and she told him that she came over on a boat. Knowing that James had the only boat, and knowing what his price was, John was incensed, so he kicked Jane out.

Jane went to the park and sat down on a bench to cry. Billy, a friend from high school, came by and asked her why she was crying. When she told him the story, Billy went and found John and punched him out.

Rank the people in the story in terms of who did the most ethical thing.

        _____Jane
        _____John
        _____Billy
        _____James
        _____Wilbur

138

Listening Exercise

Jane and John

Divide up into pairs. Ask your partner to explain how he or she ranked each individual and why. Do not respond while this person is explaining. You can ask questions to clarify your partner's point of view, but do not discuss or debate what he or she is saying.

Then explain how you ranked the individuals and why. Your partner may ask questions for clarification but may not debate or discuss your ranking.

When you have finished this, then repeat back to your partner how he or she ranked the individuals and why.

Then have your partner do the same.

After the class partners have completed their ranking and sharing, the entire class will come together to share their experiences. The focus of the discussion should be on the challenge of listening openly when others have different viewpoints.

Option III - Important People in My Life

Students will have the opportunity to identify who in their lives has contributed to their ethical and personal development. This activity not only facilitates students considering what significant individuals have influenced their lives but specifically what they have learned or observed in others that has become central to who they are today.

Students will make a Six-Pointed Star (identical in shape to the Star of David) on a sheet of paper. Within the triangle shape of each point, the students should write the name of a person who has helped shape their development and values. At the tip of each point in the star the students write the value(s) that they believe they learned from the person written in the triangle portion of the star. For example, a student might write down the name of "Uncle Teddy" because the student learned the importance of "working hard for anything that I really want" from that uncle.

After the students have completed their star with the names of the influential persons and what they have learned, they should get into dyads or triads and share what they have recorded on their star. Give students time to discuss and share with one another.

This might be an activity that you as the instructor would collect and review because it can be a valuable tool in getting to know the students in the class on a deeper level.

Journaling Activities

My educational goals are fueled by my belief that...

I believe that I have been an influential person in the life of ...

I think I have made a difference to this person by...

I am discouraged about America's future when I see...

I am encouraged about America's future when I see...

Evaluating Student Mastery and Application
Chapter 8

Objective Test Questions.

1. A person who has personal integrity is
   a. Someone who others find trustworthy.
   b. Someone who follows what his or her parents taught him or her.
   c. Someone who does not make mistakes.
   d. a. and c.

2. According to Brown's Model for the Ethical Processing in a group, which one of the following is not a key step in working through a decision?
   a. Establish what needs to be accomplished.
   b. Explore hidden agendas or invalidated assumptions.
   c. Assess the cost of the decision.
   d. Determine what is important.

3. Values are to the principles accepted by a person as ethics are to
   a. A commitment to honesty.
   b. The rules guiding one's conduct.
   c. The religious beliefs of a person.
   d. The relationship that a person maintains with another person.

4. A person who is demonstrating initiative might be seen doing which of the following?
   a. Getting started in achieving goals.
   b. Reflecting over how well he or she has achieved goals.
   c. Considering the guidelines for working within a community.
   d. Giving his or her opinion on how to most effectively start a project.
   e. All of the above.

5. Failure could be an even more negative circumstance in one's life if he or she
   a. Shares his or her experience with others.
   b. Allows the failure to shape his or her self concept.
   c. Spends time trying to figure out why the failure occurred.
   d. Considers what personal limitations may have contributed to the failure.

6. Motivation involves which of the following steps?
   a. Deciding what you want to achieve
   b. Getting moving toward your goal and taking the initial step
   c. Eliminating anything that might hold you back from achieving your goal
   d. All of the above
   e. All of the above except c.

Essay and Short Answer.

Give an example from your own life of how you have recently attempted to be a person of integrity in the following areas.

Moral Principle_____

_____

_____

Honesty_____

_____

_____

Sincerity_____

_____

_____

Consideration for Others _____

_____

_____

Essay. Illustrate how a company department might select a charity to support for an office service project. Use the Brown Model for Ethical Processing in a step by step analysis.

_____

Key For Objective Test Questions.

1. e.
2. c.
3. b.
4. a.
5. b.
6. e.

References

Hunter, Lewis (1990). *A Question of Values.* San Franciso:HarperCollins Publishers.

Palmer, Parker (1990). *The Active Life*. New York: HarperCollins Publishers.

The People Connection: Relating to Others
Chapter 9

Key Concepts: A myriad of issues concerning communication skills and developing healthy relationships is discussed in this chapter. Students not only explore interpersonal relationships but also their involvement in the larger community. The topics of diversity and individual differences are highlighted as issues that are particularly critical for students today.

Additional Ideas to Explore with Students: In general, relationships are a strong priority in the lives of college students. Initiating college friendships and relationships, understanding how to relate to others as an independent adult, and appreciating differences between people are skills that students need to learn and practice. In addition, traditional-aged students are usually negotiating their roles and responsibilities within their family of origin. At the same time, older students find themselves redefining their expectations with their adult friends, spouses, and in some cases, their children.

Particularly, younger students (but in some cases, the older students) believe that starting "fresh" at college means that the difficulties they have experienced in the past will no longer be problematic. The reality is that their old relational patterns of communicating generally have not been altered from within. If a short temper got them in trouble in the past, it probably will flare up again. If shyness made meeting people challenging, the likelihood is that making new friends will still be intimidating. And if trusting in others has been an obstacle in the past, then new faces will not erase their reticence. The relationship patterns that individuals make growing up are often repeated as adults. This is a relatively new concept for college students, but psychologists, in particular family therapists, have noted these patterns for some time. Making changes in communication patterns requires self-examination and skill building.

College students are usually learning how to relate to a much wider variety of people than they may have known in their hometown or high school. This wider variety of people represents more diverse cultures and at times even opposing points of view. It is a process of learning how to communicate that can be somewhat threatening for some college students. Discovering that the ideas and beliefs that others hold do not need to diminish their own beliefs and ideas is a significant awareness for many college students. Learning how to respect these differences and also how to express their own ideas are critical skills for the young adult to acquire.

Individual Assignments

Option I - Interview with an International Student

Many college students do not take the opportunity to get to know the international students on the campus. By not taking the time to get to know the international students, American students miss out on a wealth of information and insight not only about other countries but also the United States. Sometimes American students need the nudge that this assignment provides to become more comfortable interacting with international students. The International Student Services Office on the campus may be very helpful in arranging this activity. The office may even be able to provide some names of students who would be willing to be interviewed by an American student.

Students are to meet in pairs with an international student for at least 30-60 minutes. The students should come to the meeting with a few questions but hopefully most of the interaction can be somewhat freewheeling and natural. During the time together, the American students should also solicit any questions from the international student concerning their adjustment to and observations of the United States. If there are any international students in the class, then they could be paired up with members of the class or directed to meet with another American student of their choice.

After the students have had their interview, they should write a one-page reaction paper about their experience. What did they find out about the international student?What were some of the adjustments that the international student experienced coming to America? Were there any observations about Americans that came as a surprise to the student conducting the interview?

Spend some time in the class debriefing the experiences that students had in their various interviews.

Option II - Information Interview

This activity is designed to assist students in learning about the value of networking. Students will be assigned to conduct an information interview with someone who is working in a professional field that they are considering pursuing. Before giving this assignment, it can be quite interesting to illustrate how close a career contact can be. Ask the students to think of a profession or career option that is relatively unique. For example, a forest ranger or a professional ski instructor could be possible suggestions that could come from the students in the class. Each student should share their career choice with the rest of the students. Then ask the students if anyone in the class personally knows someone in the profession identified by a student. If no one knows someone personally who is in a given profession, then ask if they know someone who knows someone who is in the given profession. You can anticipate that within a class of at least 20-30 students, there will be a professional contact within two "relationships" of someone in the class for most professions. This is a persuasive illustration of the availability of network contacts even among family and friends.

Next, students set up an interview with someone who is in or has been in a career that the students have an interest in pursuing and learning more about. The campus Career Center can be a helpful resource and may have names of alumni that are very willing to be interviewed by students. Students should write the answers to the questions on the sheet that follows.

Information Interview

Date of interview _____

Name of the professional interviewed and his/her profession_____
_____

What do you like about your profession?_____
_____
_____

What do you not like about your profession?_____
_____
_____

What educational training do you need to succeed in this profession? What skills are essential for this profession?_____
_____
_____

Would you recommend this profession to others? Why or why not?_____
_____
_____

What is a typical professional day like for you? What types of things do you do on most days?_____
_____
_____

How do you see the profession changing over the next three to five years?

_____
_____
_____

Questions for the student to answer based on the interview.

Has this interview changed your ideas or assumptions about this profession?

_____

_____

Were there any surprises in that you learned from this interview?

_____

Has this interview adjusted your career direction at all?
Explain._____

Option III - Campus Resources

Students often overlook the many resources that are available to them. This activity encourages students to uncover some of the **key people and offices** that could be invaluable to their college success. Students will uncover some of the hidden networks (or at least some of the less obvious contacts) around the campus. First, students complete the following form on campus referrals and resources. Some of these resources can be found by checking the University Phone Directory, the Campus Home Page, the Student Handbook and other special interest brochures and pamphlets. But one of the most valuable ways to discover the best resources is to ask other students, especially upper classman.

When students have completed their hunt for campus resources and completed the form, it will be beneficial to take some time in class comparing notes. Have students compile a master list that can be copied and distributed to the entire class. Have students share how they found their leads on some of the resources. If students appear to have had some difficulty locating any specific campus resources, be certain to offer some options for them to note.

Campus Resources

Include the name, phone number and location of all of the resources that you have uncovered. A particularly helpful publication or computer network resource could also be included.

Where could you get information about what classes to take next term?

a._____

b._____

c._____

Where could you find out about campus clubs and organizations?

a._____

b._____

c._____

Where could you get information about jobs off campus?

a._____

b._____

c._____

Where could you get information about babysitters or child care?

a._____

b._____

c._____

Where could you find out about car-pooling with someone?

a._____

b._____

c._____

Where could you get some information about declaring a major?

    a._____

    b._____

    c._____

Where could you get information about a support group or counseling group?

    a._____

    b._____

    c._____

Where could you get information about the opportunities for religious or spiritual fellowship?

    a._____

    b._____

    c._____

Classroom Activities

Option I - Different Cultures

This activity is a relatively non-threatening way to explore different cultures in a group. Through this exercise, students will become more aware of the human tendency to view others through the "lenses" of their culture and experience. These personal "lenses" filter their perceptions about others. People view one another through the filters of family upbringing, gender, ethnicity, religion, and community. Often travel facilitates a greater awareness of the cultural differences between people because some of the filters are at least temporarily removed. This activity uses a series of pictures depicting various cultures as a way to become more aware of American "lenses".

To begin, pictures from a periodical like *National Geographic* are collected. The pictures selected should feature people from cultures different from the mainstream American culture. The pictures could show people involved with ceremonies, rituals, and interactions that are different from what most Americans experience. The more unique the situation depicted, the better. Cut out the pictures and delete any explanations of what is going on in the picture. Then mount the pictures on sturdy paper or make them into slides so you can use them again.

This activity should be done individually and then shared with partners. Distribute a card for the students to record their observations about the picture. Show the pictures to the students and have them answer the following questions about each picture.

> **1. What do I observe in this picture?** Students should only focus
> on the physical or visual cues in the picture.
>
> **2. What do I think is happening in this picture?** Students
> interpret what they think is happening in the picture.
>
> **3. Why do I interpret this meaning for the picture? What
> have I experienced that makes me think this is happening?**
> Students consider the filters that they use to interpret the picture.

After the students have written their responses to the 5-10 pictures that have been shown, the class shares their individual and dyad perceptions. Go back through the pictures and tell the students what is actually occurring in each picture. Before presenting the correct interpretation of the picture, take some time to hear the students' guesses and what clues they used to make their guesses and how their background influences their perceptions. Use the discussion to process the concept of cultural filters and how those filters contribute to our misunderstandings of one another.

Continue discussing the examples of times the students became more aware of their own biases and cultural filters when traveling outside the United States. This can also be an excellent opportunity to solicit the experiences that international students have had since coming to the states. Illustrations about the dating patterns, family expectations and higher education could be good launching points for this discussion. International students should be encouraged to share their first impressions of Americans. What assumptions did the international students have about American college students? Did any of their assumptions prove to be untrue once they got to know the American college students better? How did their "lenses" influence their assumptions and impressions?

Option II - Winter Survival

This activity provides students with an interesting decision-making activity that illustrates the demands and the value of using consensus building. It is a "classic" exercise taken from an outstanding resource, <u>Joining Together</u> written by Johnson and Johnson.

Students initially rank the items that would be useful to the survivors of a winter airplane crash. Then students work together in groups of 5-7 to determine jointly what items would be most useful to the victims of the crash. In almost every situation, students will find that their group ranking is more similar to the "expert ranking" than their individual ranking. Before beginning the processing, select one or two persons in each group to be observers of the process within the group.

Instructions to Observers

This exercise looks at the process by which groups make decisions. Crucial issues are how well the group uses the resources of its members, how much commitment to implement the decision is mustered, how the future decision-making ability of the group is affected and how members feel about and react to what is taking place. As an observer, the observer should focus on the following issues:

1. Who does and does not participate in the discussion? Who participates the most and who does not? How is influence determined (expertise, gender, loudness of voice)? What roles do the members take?

2. Who is involved and who is not involved?

3. How did the group handle conflict? How were decisions made?

4. How did leadership emerge in the group?

5. What types of thinking were people using? Use the Thinktrix Model.

Students begin by reading the following scenario and then making their determinations about what items would be most critical to survival of the crash victims.

Winter Survival Exercise

You have just crash-landed in the woods of northern Minnesota and southern Manitoba. It is 11:32 a.m. in mid-January. The light plane in which you were traveling crashed on a lake. The pilot and the co-pilot were killed. Shortly after the crash the plane sank completely into the lake with the pilot's and the co-pilot's bodies inside. None of you is seriously injured and you are all dry.

The crash came suddenly, before the pilot had time to radio for help or to inform anyone of your position. Since your pilot was trying to avoid a storm, you know the plane was considerably off course. The pilot announced shortly before the crash that you were twenty miles northwest of a small town that is the nearest known habitation.

You are in a wilderness area made up of thick woods broken by many lakes and streams. The snow depth varies from above the ankles to knee-deep where it drifted. The last weather report indicated that the temperature would reach minus twenty-five degrees fahrenheit in the daytime and minus forty at night. There is plenty of dead wood and twigs in the immediate area. You are dressed in winter clothing appropriate for city wear.

While escaping from the plane the several members of your group salvaged twelve items. Your task is to rank these items according to their importance to your survival, starting with 1 for the most important item and ending with 12 for the least important one.

You may assume that the number of passengers is the same as the number of persons in your group, and that the group has agreed to stick together.

Winter Survival Decision Form

Rank the following items according to their importance to your survival, starting with 1 for the most important and proceeding to 12 for the least important one.

_____Ball of steel wool

_____Newspapers (one per person)

_____Compass

_____Hand Ax

_____Cigarette lighter (without fluid)

_____Loaded .45 caliber pistol

_____Sectional air map made of plastic

_____Twenty-by-twenty foot piece of heavy-duty canvas

_____Extra shirt and pants for each survivor

_____Can of shortening

_____Quart of 100-proof whiskey

_____Family-size chocolate bar (one per person)

After everyone has completed their individual form, the group comes together to share their ideas. The goal of the group is to use a consensus decision process to determine what the best group ranking can be. There should be no voting but instead discussion from all members to jointly determine how to accomplish the ranking. All members should be solicited for their opinions and perspectives.

When the group has made its decisions, the group members are given the ranking that has been determined by the "experts". Group members may want to check and see if their group ranking matched the expert ranking better than the individual ranking.

Finally, group members take time to discuss how well they worked together and to get feedback from the observers. During the debriefing the group members should focus on what they noted about how the group worked together and how well positive communication skills were practiced.

Key for Expert Ranking
_2_ Ball of steel wool
_8_ Newspapers (one per person)
_12_ Compass
_6_ Hand Ax
_1_ Cigarette lighter (without fluid)
_9_ Loaded .45 caliber pistol
_11_ Sectional air map made of plastic
_5_ Twenty-by-twenty foot piece of heavy duty canvas
_3_ Extra shirt and pants for each survivor
_4_ Can of shortening
_10_ Quart of 100-proof whiskey
_7_ Family-size chocolate bar (one per person)

Journaling Activities

One area that I would like to be more effective in my communication skills is...

The way I believe that I contribute to groups is...

I am concerned that others may at times perceive me to be...

One person that I would like to get to know and understand better is...

Ways that I could open up my communication with this person is by...

Evaluating Student Mastery and Application
Chapter 9

Objective Exam Questions

1. Typically a person who is trying to understand what someone else is communicating or saying is
    a. Encoding
    b. Decoding
    c. Transmitting
    d. Conceptualizing

2. The communication process of interpreting a message from another person is
    a. Responding
    b. Decoding
    c. Receiving
    d. Transmitting

3. When encoding occurs in the Communication Loop, a person is
    a. Telling someone his/her ideas.
    b. Hearing the message from someone else.
    c. Determining how to express his/her ideas.
    d. Interpreting the ideas of someone else.

4. Aggressive communicators may express their ideas and feelings by
    a. Belittling the ideas expressed by others.
    b. Intimidating others into their point of view.
    c. Leaving the room before the disagreement is resolved.
    d. Becoming physically abusive.
    e. All of the above.

5. An individual's race is evident in
    a. Physical characteristics that are genetically transmitted.
    b. Vocabulary and dialect.
    c. National citizenship.
    d. Cultural and/or religious traditions.
    e. All of the above.

6. Non-verbal communication works in tandem with verbal communication when
    a. The verbal and the non-verbal expressions are congruent.
    b. The speaker moves as close as possible to the listener.
    c. The non-verbal communication is not visible to the listener.
    d. Eye contact is maintained regardless of who the listener may be.
    e. All of the above.

7. Which of the following is an example of good communication
    a. "You are such always late!"
    b. "If it's what you want it doesn't matter what I want."
    c. "Men are just more competitive than women."
    d. "I feel so disappointed that you forgot my birthday."
    e. b. and d.

8. Discrimination is demonstrated in which of the following situations
    a. Someone is not hired because he or she is just three years away from retirement.
    b. A woman is not promoted because she might get pregnant within the next few years.
    c. A male is not hired because he won't feel comfortable in an all female department.
    d. A disabled person is not accepted into a sales position because he or she might not be able to keep up the pace.
    e. All of the above.
    f. None of the above.

Essay and Short Answer.

Describe at least five barriers to clear communication that can occur between the speaker and the listener.

_____
_____
_____
_____
_____
_____
_____

Key to Objective Questions

1. b.
2. b.
3. c.
4. e.
5. a.
6. a.
7. d.
8. e.

References

Banks, James A. & Banks, Cherry A, McGee (1993) *Multicultural Education*. Boston, MA.: Allyn and Bacon.

Bennett, Christine (1990) *Comprehensive Multicultural Education*. Boston, MA.: Allyn and Bacon.

Ford, Clyde W. (1994). *We Can All Get Along*. New York: Bantam Doubleday Publishing Group Inc..

Katzenbach, Jon & Smith, Douglas (1993). *The Wisdom of Teams*. New York: McKinsey and Company, Inc.

Johnson, David & Johnson (199). *JoiningTogether*. New York: Prentice Hall.

Lerner, Harriet Goldhor (1985). *The Dance of Anger*. New York: Harper & Row Publishers, Inc..

McGinnis, Alan Loy (1979). *The Friendship Factor*. Minneapolis, MI: Angsburg Publishing House

Films and Videos for Class Use.

ColdWater
> *Distributed by the International Student Office, Boston University, 19 Deerfield St. Boston, MA 02215*
> *A one hour video that highlights international students and their adjustments to the United States.*

Skin Deep
> *Distributed by Iris Films, 2600 10th Street, Suite 413, Berkley, CA 95710*
> *A 53 minute video that chronicles the journey of a diverse group of college students as they examine their attitude and prejudices.*

Reality Resources: Managing Your Finances and Work
Chapter 10

Key concepts: Managing personal finances and resources are the topics discussed in Chapter 10. Practical information about banking, budgeting and using credit is explored to assist students in making responsible choices about their finances.

Additional Information for Exploration with Students: In decades past, students who left college identified financial difficulties as the primary reason for leaving the campus. Most educational researchers agreed that in fact "financial problems" were not the actual reason that the students dropped out. Instead, the researchers discovered that the financial issues were rarely the real reason for students' decisions to exit from the campus. However, during the last decade the educational researchers agree that finances and the cost of education are now the most significant reason that students are dropping out of colleges and universities. Spiraling tuition costs and diminishing state and federal financial aid have resulted in a student population that is truly anxious about finances.

Today, students are frequently financing their education by working extensive hours while trying to go to school. Most students are taking more than four years to complete their education. In fact, a minority of students actually complete their Bachelor's degree within the traditional four years. In addition, students are taking out significant loans to finance their education. According to national financial aid records, the average total educational loan for students earning their baccalaureate degree is over $5,000.

Many students have had minimal experience handling their finances at home and find budgeting money and handling bills a daunting task or at least a confusing one. This chapter helps take some of the mystery out of money management.

Individual Assignments

Option I - Monitoring Expenses

Most students, and for that matter most adults, are not very aware of where their money goes on a daily basis. A pizza, a movie ticket, and a paperback book add up to much more than most individuals believe is possible. This activity requires that students track all of their expenses for one week. It is anticipated that students will be somewhat surprised at how much all of the little incidentals and impulse purchases cost them during a week.

Probably the easiest way to conduct this expense monitor is have students keep a small envelope in their pocket book, back pack or pocket with a small pad of paper or a few three-by-five cards to record their expenses. Even cans of soda from the vending machine should be included in this expense monitoring.

At the end of the week, students should tabulate their expenses by category and also as a total figure. Categories for maintaining expenses are as follows:

1. Food
2. Clothing and personal items
3. Entertainment, Cultural events
4. Car expenses
5. Commuting costs (bus, ferry, parking, gas)
6. Medical care
7. Child care
8. Books, labs, fees
9. Gifts and cards
10. Miscellaneous

Students complete the Expense Summary on the next page.

Expense Summary

Categories of Expenses:

Food
        Restaurant/Eating Out
        Groceries   _____

Clothing, laundry and personal care   _____

Entertainment and Cultural events   _____

Child Care   _____

Car expenses   _____

Books, lab fees, school supplies   _____

Commuting costs (gas, bus, car pool cost, parking)   _____

Gifts, cards,   _____

Medical and dental care   _____

Miscellaneous   _____

Total   _____

As you look over your expenses, are there any surprises? Explain.

_____

_____

_____

Are there some areas of expenses that are more or less than you anticipated?

_____

_____

Is there a need to make some adjustments in how you spend money? Explain.

_____

_____

_____

Option II - Campus Network

Students often overlook the multitude of resources that are available to them right on their campus. This activity encourages students to uncover some of those resources. Students will complete the form on campus resources and referrals. Some of the best resources may in fact be the ones that are not publicized in a formal sense.

The resource people that students identify can be found through a number of sources including the University Phone Directory, the Campus Home Page, the Student Handbook and campus brochures. One of the best ways to find good resource people is to ask other students, particularly upper-classmen.

Career testing, physical check-ups, fitness evaluations and resume critiques are generally offered on the campus at minimal or no charge to the students. It is important that students recognize that many of these types of services would be at a significant cost to them if they were not students at a university or college.

Campus Resources

Include a phone number, campus location and any special charges in your resource listing.

Who or what office could help you select classes?

_____
_____
_____

Who or what office could help you find out about campus clubs and organizations?

_____
_____
_____

Who or what office could assist you in applying to graduate schools?

_____
_____
_____

Who or what office could help you find child care or baby-sitting referrals?

_____
_____
_____

Who or what office could help you locate commuting and car pool information?

_____
_____
_____

Who or what office could be of assistance in locating a religious or spiritual fellowship opportunity?

_____
_____

Who or what office could get you "in the know" about exercise, fitness or intramural options on the campus?

_____
_____
_____

Classroom Activities

Option I - Bargain Hunt

In general, students are on a relatively modest income. Fortunately, most students share this financial limitation. Finding ways to stretch their budget can seem embarrassing or uncomfortable for many students. This assignment may ease some of the stresses of finances by discovering some of the places and programs around the community and campus that offer a "good buy" for the money. Also, students may feel reassured that they are not alone in their financial concerns. This activity is a "Bargain Hunt" that is conducted by the students in dyads or triads.

Students have one week to find as many "bargains" as they can in the various categories that are listed on the "Bargain Hunt" form. The students can use the phone book, newspapers, books, or personal recommendations to gather their resources. Some, but not necessarily all, of the recommendations may be available just for college students. For example, many theaters have tickets for students at half price that are sold one hour before the performance for any seats that are still not sold. Some museums have one day a week that is designated as a free admission day.

Have the students share their "best bargains" with the rest of class. It might be fun to give a prize for the best "Sale Sleuth" team.

Bargain Hunt

List the names, phone numbers and locations for each of the bargains that are listed.

1. Cheap Eats

_____

_____

_____

2. Clothing on a Shoestring

_____

_____

_____

3. Health and Personal supplies

_____

_____

_____

4. Books and School Supplies

_____

_____

_____

5. Computer supplies, media, appliances

_____

_____

_____

6. Tapes and C.D.'s

_____

_____

7. Entertainment, Sports and Cultural Events

_____

_____

_____

_____

8. Other bargains worth pursuing

_____

_____

_____

Option II - Alumni Panel

It can be very beneficial for students to learn from those who have successfully graduated and are currently launching careers or attending graduate school. In part, the alumni can also encourage students by letting them know that "they can do it". The Career Development Office or the Alumni Office of your campus may be very supportive in setting up the panel of alumni.

Invite 3-5 alumni from very different careers and disciplines to come to the class to share their experiences. Be sure to be sensitive to a gender and ethnic mix in your panel membership. Alumni in all likelihood should be prepared with some questions to get the discussion launched. But students in the class should also be encouraged to ask questions of the alumni panel.

Some questions that you might want to give to the panel members before they arrive include any of the following:

a. What was your biggest transition from school to work?

b. How did you decide upon your current vocation and major?

c. How did you locate and apply for your current position?

d. Have you faced any ethical or professional dilemmas that were confusing or very challenging?

e. In retrospect, what do you wish you had done differently while you were a student?

f. What advice do you have for college students today that will help them make the transition to the world of work go more smoothly?

Journaling Activities

How does money relate to my personal sense of worth?

What does money mean to me?

As far as money goes, do I feel "one up" or "one down" with those around me?

Three people that really believe in me are...

Three people that I believe would write a positive recommendation for a job application are...

Three people that I believe would write a positive recommendation for an educational program, admissions or scholarships are...

Evaluating Student Mastery and Application

Objective Test Questions

1. Which of the following statements is true of the educational choices of students today?
   a. There are more working students today than in 1980
   b. Almost 60% of undergraduate students work at least part-time during the year.
   c. Students are most frequently employed in service and administrative support positions.
   d. More students are going to college full-time so they can complete their education quickly.
   e. a. and c.
   f. a. and d.

2. The Perkins Loan offered by the federal government is
   a. Not a need-based loan.
   b. Considers outstanding academic performance.
   c. Offers a grace period for repayment after graduation.
   d. Is issued through the state government administration.
   e. All of the above.

3. Students who work while attending school are advised to consider what factors?
   a. How the job meets their long-term career aspirations.
   b. Whether the hours work well with their class schedule.
   c. How the job fulfills their financial needs for school and living costs.
   d. All of the above.

4. The SEOG (Supplemental Educational Opportunity Grant) is different from the Pell Grant because
   a. The Pell Grant is administered by the school and the SEOG Grant is not.
   b. The SEOG is administered by the school and the Pell Grant is not.
   c. The SEOG recognizes scholarship and Pell Grant does not.
   d. The Pell Grant recognizes scholarship and the SEOG does not.

5. Federal Grants are only given to students
   a. Who have exceptional talent and academic records.
   b. With the understanding that a percentage of the grant will be repaid.
   c. Who are undergraduate students.
   d. Who are willing to work while they are attending school.
   e. None of the above.

6. Networking is not
    a. a one-time interview meeting.
    b. useful to find job openings.
    c. useful for ruling out certain companies from your job search.
    d. helpful in finding additional referrals.
    e. None of the above.

7. Which of the following statements is true?
    a. Students who do not work at all earn the best grades.
    b. The number of students who work full-time is on the decline.
    c. Students can make valuable professional contacts when they work.
    d. Students who work at a work study position can work 40 hours a week at that job.
    e. a. and c.
    f. b. and c.

8. Which of the following statements about the Stafford Loan Program is true?
    a. In some cases, the interest is subsidized by the government.
    b. Requires that students attend school full-time.
    c. Has a uniform interest rate for all students.
    d. Has an established deadline application date.
    e. All of the above.

Essay and Short Answer.

Essay. List five sources that can give you good leads for current or potential job openings.

_____
_____
_____
_____
_____

Essay. Assume that your younger brother plans to start college next year and asks you for your advice on whether he should get a job while he is a student. What are some of the considerations that you would highlight for him in making his decision?

_____
_____
_____
_____
_____
_____
_____

Key to Objective Test Questions

1. e.
2. c.
3. d.
4. b.
5. e.
6. a.
7. c.
8. a.

References

Dominguez, Joe & Robin, Vicki (1994). *Your Money or YourLife: Transforming Your Relationship with Money and Achieving Financial Independence.* New York: Viking Penguin.

Elgin, Duane (1981). *Voluntary Simplicity.* New York: Marrow.

Porter, Sylvia (1990). *Sylvia Porter's Your Financial Security.* New York: Avon.

Savage, Terry (1993). *New Money Strategies for the 90's.* New York:HarperCollins Publishers, Inc..

Your Life: Moving Ahead
Chapter 11

Key Concepts: This concluding chapter offers a capstone to the information and ideas discussed in the earlier chapters. Authors Carter and Kravits focus on the future lifestyle disciplines and priorities that students are beginning to develop. Suggestions for sustaining personal motivation and momentum throughout one's life are highlighted.

Additional Ideas to Explore with Students: The first term of college is a major adjustment for students - new expectations, new freedoms, and new relationships. The number of changes and choices create one of the most demanding life transitions. Generally, the first term of college is essentially a time of personal survival. Once students have settled into positive relationships and routines, some predictability and stability begins to emerge in their lives. By the end of their first year of college, most students begin to feel that they are capable of succeeding academically and personally. It is no accident that the most critical period for student retention is the very first term. For some the challenges and changes prove to be too much. That is why this course is so critical.

The conclusion of the course offers an occasion for students to take stock and refocus their energies. It is also a time to cement the skills and concepts that have been discussed during the class. And finally, it is a time for the students to experience a sense of closure and connection. It is important that there be an opportunity for students to evaluate the course and to give some feedback and encouragement to one another.

Individual Assignments

Option I a - Personal Reflection Paper

Students write a two- to three-page paper that explores the ways they believe they have changed or grown since beginning college. Papers should include specific examples of who or what has affected their beliefs and behaviors. Students may want to describe some learning that has occurred from a positive recognition or accomplishment, but they may also want to share some things that they have learned "the hard way". In some cases, their learning may reflect concepts and skills that they have had to <u>relearn</u>. The paper should highlight at least two to three changes that have occurred thus far in their college experience.

Option I b - Reflections on a Quotation

Students write a two- to three-page paper that explores how one of the following quotations captures the personal growth they have experienced since beginning college. Specific illustrations and examples should accompany the students's examination of the way(s) they have changed or matured. If none of the quotes appears to be applicable, the students may select a quote of their own determination.

"Every time you don't follow your inner guidance, you feel a loss of energy, loss of power, a sense of spiritual deadness."

Shataki Gawain

"To live a creative life, we must lose our fear of being wrong."

Joseph Chilton Pearce

"Do not fear mistakes - there are none."

Miles Davis

"In the middle of the difficulty lies the opportunity."

Albert Einstein

"You need to claim the events of your life to make yourself yours."

Anne Wilson-Schaff

"Every beginning ends something."

Paul Valery

"I don't know the key to success, but the key to failure is trying to please everybody."

Bill Cosby

Option II - Doing Something on the Edge

It's easy to fall into a routine. We drive the same way to work or school. We eat what we know we like. We watch the same television shows. Sometimes by placing oneself into a new activity or relationship, it is possible to gain a new perspective on oneself and the world. Trying something new may require some extraordinary courage and commitment. In almost every case, the intentionality of trying something that is unknown facilitates a feeling of similarities and accomplishment.

Students are to identify some activity or experience that they have never tried before. This assignment requires that students determine something new to try and then to attempt the activity or experience. Third, students complete the "Reflections From the Edge" form that is on the next page. Some types of activities that students could consider include the following:

*Attend a church or temple religious service different from what you have attended.

*Attempt some physical activity like riding a bike 20 miles, running a 10K Race, or snorkeling.

*Try foods from a country or ethnic menu that you have never tried.

*Go to the Opera.

*Serve food at a Soup Kitchen.

*Country Line Dancing

*Be alone for 24 hours

*Draw a picture

*Take an auto mechanics class

*Audition for a part in a play

*Try skiing or skating

Reflections From the Edge

What activity did you select? Where did you go? Did you make any special arrangements? Did you engage someone to teach you how to do the activity?

_____
_____
_____
_____

Why did you select the activity or experience that you did? Why do you believe that you have not tried this activity before?

_____
_____
_____

How did you feel about the experience that you tried? Would you do it again?
What skills did you use to participate in this activity?

_____
_____
_____
_____
_____

What did you learn about yourself from this experience?

_____
_____
_____
_____
_____

Would you do this activity again? Why or why not?

_____
_____
_____
_____

Option III - A Future Goal

Students have no doubt learned a lot about themselves during this academic term. Based on what they have learned and how they would like to grow in the future, students write one specific goal for the upcoming term. Students will establish one specific goal that they would like to achieve. The goal may be some discipline that they have allowed to lapse but would like to rekindle. On the other hand, the goal may be a new discipline or direction that could be initiated during the next term.

The goal should be **specific** and **measurable.** Furthermore, the goal should include an **action plan** and how the student will attempt to be **accountable**. After the students have written their goal, they should seal it in a pre-addressed envelope and give it to you at the end of the academic term. Within 5-10 weeks, you mail the goal back to students so they can check how they are progressing in the accomplishment of their personal goal.

Classroom Activities

Option I - Course Evaluation

While your university or college may already have a course evaluation procedure in place, it may be beneficial to include some process questions regarding the strengths of the class and areas that need improvement. The use of written anecdotal observations may be somewhat threatening to some students who may fear writing anything challenging or critical because they fear their comments could negatively affect their grade.

Therefore, it would be helpful to have a person that is not connected to the class collect the comments written by students. Then this person could either synthesize the results of the students' comments in an evaluation summary report or the student evaluations could be given to the instructor after the class grades have been submitted.

Suggested evaluation questions include the following:

What was the most helpful or beneficial concept or skill have you learned from this class?

What was the least helpful or beneficial about this class?

How did the instructor promote your learning?

Did the instructor do anything that inhibited or discouraged your learning?

Were the class sessions well organized and interesting?

How did the textbook support and enhance your learning in this class? Any suggestions you can make to improve the textbook?

Were the methods for evaluating student mastery of the concepts useful, clear and fair? If not, give examples of changes you would make for improvement?

Which assignments were most useful and meaningful for you?

How did you perceive the classroom environment? Did the instructor encourage student participation and questions? How? If not, what would have been helpful?

Were all students treated with respect and fairness?

Option II - Sharing Affirmations

This assignment may or may not be appropriate depending on the size of the class and the sharing that has occurred among class participants throughout the term. If you do not believe that the students know each other very well or see this activity as somewhat contrived, you may want to consider an alternative way to encourage affirmation and feedback between students.

In this activity, the instructor writes the names of each student in the class on three different cards. For example, if the class has twenty students there should be sixty total cards. Then the students draw the names of three different students that have been in the class. Each student is instructed to write at least one affirmation on each card for each of the three students that they have drawn. If the student does not know one of the students they have drawn, they may either trade with a classmate or write something that they have observed about the way the student participates in the class. For example, the feedback might be "I appreciated the comment you made about ----" or "I'm glad you asked the question that you did about the exam because I had the same concern."

The instructor collects all of the cards and reviews them before placing them in an envelope that is addressed to the student. If you wish to, you may want to add your feedback card to the envelope. It would be most appropriate that if you do write feedback cards, it should be done for all of the students. Distribute the envelopes to students with the three or four affirmations in each envelope. A meaningful discussion could be conducted about the importance of affirmation and how to share constructive affirmations.

Journaling Activities

This term, I am proud that I have accomplished...

Since the beginning of the term, my friendships (relationships) have changed....

I feel best about myself when I am...

I feel worst about myself when I am...

My values (spiritual commitments) have changed or grown ...

This term, the sense of balance in my life has...

Student Mastery and Application
Chapter 11

Objective Test Questions

1. Which of the following is not a recommendation for continued personal growth and renewal?
   - a. Appreciate the creative efforts of others.
   - b. Change careers often for stimulation.
   - c. Experience some spiritual pursuits.
   - d. Travel and learn about other cultures.
   - e. Create something even if you are not an "artist".

2. In order for criticism to be constructive it should
   - a. be offered in general, non-specific ways.
   - b. Be aired immediately so things can get out in the open.
   - c. Describe how the behavior impacts the recipient.
   - d. Offer assistance for changing of the behavior.
   - e. All of the above.

3. When receiving feedback or criticism it is helpful to
   - a. State the feedback as you think you have heard it.
   - b. Solicit suggestions for how to make the changes in the criticized behavior.
   - c. Resist the temptation to explain or defend your behavior.
   - d. Ask for specific examples of how the behavior is seen.
   - e. All of the above.

4. What are some ways that you can demonstrate your concern for the environment?
   - a. Recycle whenever possible.
   - b. Reuse whatever you can.
   - c. Be kind to the environment.
   - d. All of the above.

5. What follows next in the problem-solving model after one has brainstormed various options for responding to the problem or concern?
   - a. Conduct an evaluation of the option selected.
   - b. Analyze the problem.
   - c. Get others involved for support.
   - d. Explore the benefits and negative results of the possible responses.

Essay. Write a draft of your life mission. Then describe one thing that you are doing today and one thing that you plan to do in the future to stay true to your mission.

_____

_____

_____

_____

_____

_____

What have you done to make a difference on the campus since you began studying at this college or university? Explain.

_____

_____

_____

_____

_____

Key to Objective Test Questions.

1. b.
2. c.
3. e.
4. e.
5. d

Future Reading Suggestions for Students:

Covey, Stephen (1994). *First Things First*. New York: Simon & Schuster Inc..

DePree, Max (1992). *Leadership Jazz*. New York: Dell Publishing.

Palmer, Parker (1990). *The Active Life*. New York: Harper & Row,
    Publishers, Inc..

Senge, Peter M. (1990) *The Fifth Discipline*. New York: Doubleday.

Best Teaching Strategies

Good teachers learn from one another as well from as their students. This Best Teaching Strategies section highlights a variety of approaches that instructors have found to be useful in their college classes. Hopefully, these practices will be informative to your teaching. Most likely all of the strategies offered will not be appropriate to all classes, all students, or for that matter all instructors. You are invited to experiment with these teaching strategies and revise or alter as you see fit.

Most university faculty have had little, if any, formal training in teaching methods. Instead most instructors learn what works through trial and error. I encourage you to attend class sessions conducted by faculty members who are highly regarded by students and other faculty alike. In addition, it may be very meaningful to invite a colleague to attend one of your classes to give you feedback. Some campuses can provide a staff member from the Media Center so you can tape one of your class meetings. Then you can review the tape yourself or with a colleague. Also, there are a number of books and articles listed that may provide effective approaches to conducting an outstanding class.

Students today are a demanding audience. Like it or not, college students press for excellence not only in the content of a class but also the style of the communication. The wider your repertoire and resources, the more likely you will be able to broaden and deepen the minds of the students in your classes.

Launching the Class

Launching a class begins long before the first meeting with the students. You have already selected your textbook and learning objectives for the class by the time the term has begun. Now comes the relationship building between you and your class. Prior to the first session, it is advisable that you visit the classroom so you know the lay-out and resources that are available. It may be well worth your while to request a specific classroom that you believe will best meet your course needs and goals. Also, plan to duplicate more syllabi and handouts for the first session than you believe you actually need. This will be greatly appreciated by the students who may have registered late and may feel a little out of the loop already.

On the first day of class, consider the following agenda items to address with the students:

1. Explain the course objectives and expectations clearly to the students. Articulate the types of classroom interaction and guidelines that you anticipate.

2. Answer the students' questions and concerns about the course as specifically as possible. If you are uncertain about the answer to a question, let the student know that you will attempt to have an answer or decision by the next class meeting time.

3. Post your name, office hours, phone number, the class name and the meeting times on the board. If you are on E-Mail, then your E-Mail Address will be appreciated by the students.

4. Tape the first session or have a printed outline of what was covered so that the students who miss the meeting can catch up quickly and you can use your time efficiently.

5. Encourage students to find a class partner who can be a resource if they miss a session or are uncertain about an idea or assignment discussed in class.

6. Give an assignment for the next session. This establishes an early signal that this class should be taken seriously.

7. Facilitate an opportunity for students to get to know you and their fellow classmates. If you have a preference for the way students are to address you, let them know. Many first-time students experience some uncertainty about what the university protocol is on the campus.

8. Have students fill out an information card or sheet so you have the most current phone number and address. Registration materials become dated quickly because students move around so often.

9. Bring a copy of the text book(s) to the class and display briefly.

10. Review any important safety and emergency procedures.

11. Introduce some course content to the first meeting or pose a problem that typifies the course during this first meeting. This will help students get a preview of the mode of inquiry and the level of rigor they can anticipate. Announce any prerequisite experiences or courses that are expected for the successful completion of the class.

12. Set a tone that is hospitable to the students and be genuinely enthusiastic about the course content.

13. If the students are willing, request that all of the students write their name, phone number and campus address/E-Mail address on a Class Roster that can be typed, duplicated and distributed to all students in the class.

14. If there are any policies regarding cheating or plagiarism, it may be beneficial to highlight at the first session or very early in the class.

Davis, Barbara (1993). Tools for teaching. San Francisco: Jossey-Bass Books.

McKeachie, W.J. (1986). Teaching tips. (8th ed.) Lexington, MA.: Heath.

Formative Classroom Assessment

Faculty generally use examinations to assess students' comprehension, and class evaluations to determine instructional effectiveness. However, there are a number of strategies that can be used to determine the quality of the learning and the teaching. These assessments can provide valuable information about the level of student understanding and whether some instructional adjustments may be needed. According to <u>Classroom Assessment Techniques</u> by Angelo and Cross, the assessments that are used to improve the quality of the teaching and learning are *formative*. The following is a brief listing of several formative assessment techniques that require a minimum amount of class time and can be introduced into most classroom environments. Many of these strategies can offer valuable information about how students are responding to the class and the content. Instructors should be prepared for some disappointing responses and even some criticism. Nevertheless, these assessment techniques can facilitate the development of critical thinking in students and improved teaching for the instructor.

"Muddiest Point". Shortly before the end of the class session or teaching unit, students are asked to write any points or concepts that seem unclear to them. It is not important that students indicate their names on these responses but if names are collected there should be no grading penalty for a particular response. Instead, it is most helpful when students are specific about any terms or concepts they are having difficulty comprehending. Three guidelines for conducting a Muddiest Point assessment - it should be quick, there should be no penalty for the student's response, and it should be immediate. In total, the student's response time should be no longer than 2-3 minutes. An open sentence like "I am unclear about..." or "I wish we had discussed ..." or "I am confused about..." or "I would like to know more about..." are possible approaches to soliciting a response from the students. At times, it may be helpful to summarize the feedback from the class and then lead further discussion on the various muddiest points.

One-Sentence Summary. In this activity, students are asked to write a one or two sentence summary of the concepts presented in a particular lecture or unit in the reading. In most cases, the summaries could be done at the end of a class period. Several alternatives to guide students in their responses include the following:

The most important concept is...

The most useful concept is...

The point I disagree with is ...

The point I agree with is...

The concept is exemplified by...

Attendance Questions. At the beginning of class, students receive a three-by-five card. Students record their name, the date, and the answer to two-three questions posed by the instructor concerning the previous lecture or assigned reading. At first, few of the students may respond correctly to the questions, but when done on a regular basis, the students will come better prepared and begin to take note of information that they might need to know prior to the class session. This can also alert students to the key information you believe is important.

Personal Application. Students are asked to describe how they are using the concepts taught in the class. This description could illustrate how their understanding of an idea has changed since the class began or how they are applying a skill featured in the course. On occasion, a short reading or media clip might be used to facilitate students' responses.

Practice Exam. Most new college students are quite uncertain about what to expect from college level exams and tests. It can be very instructive for the students to experience the type of test questions that they might receive on a graded exam. Therefore, the practice exam can give students the chance to get a sneak preview of what the actual exam might be like. Generally, the practice exam should be not more than 25% of the actual length of the "real" exam and should have questions that are similar to the actual type of questions that are on the course exams. No penalty for the practice exam should be given and usually the students can actually "grade" their responses within the class.

Angelo, Thomas A. & Cross, K. Patricia (1993). Classroom assessment techniques. San Francisco: Jossey-Bass Books.

Creating Overheads

Many overheads (transparencies) have been provided with this textbook but no doubt you will also create your own overheads and diagrams for class use. Here are some important principles in designing effective overheads. Overheads can significantly enrich the classroom experience, particularly for visual learners. However, overheads that are crowded and unclear may only frustrate the learning process.

1. Mixed case lettering is better than all upper case or all lower case lettering.

2. Horizontal lettering is easier to read than vertical lettering.

3. Use lots of white space; don't try to cram too much information on any one overhead.

4. In general, the lettering should have no more than six lines, no more than six words per line, and be readable at six feet.

5. Think of overheads as advertising bill boards.

6. If using colored overheads, be certain that the lettering does not become too difficult to read.

7. Incorporate shapes and bullets to highlight key ideas.

8. Consider vocabulary that is appropriate to the audience.

9. Show the overhead on the screen only as long as it highlights the information you are presenting. Once you have covered the concepts on the overhead, turn off the projector to avoid distraction.

Grouping Students for Discussions

The classroom activities presented in this manual are designed for groups of 3-8. However, in most cases the optimal group size is generally 4-6 members. For most discussion exercises, the student groups should not exceed eight in total or there is a high likelihood that some group members will become reticent to share and more dependent on the vocal members of their group. Generally, the group assignments are made to create a more heterogeneous group discussion and facilitate the getting acquainted of students with one another. However, there are times when it is beneficial to create more homogeneous groups with members who share some characteristic or experience in common such as commuters vs. residential students, traditional-aged students vs. older adult learners, first-year students vs. transfer students, and so on.

Frequently, instructors utilize the reliable "counting off" method to create random group memberships. But there are a number of other possibilities for grouping that can enhance energy and productivity. Depending on the activity and classroom logistics, you may want to group students by using some interesting alternative approaches.

*Students get into discussion groups according to their living situation such as residence hall, at home with parents, an apartment, a fraternity or sorority house, etc.

*Students select a group with students that have the same major or career direction.

*Students form groups using a type of lottery whereby they draw a number or receive a candy or fruit and must get together with students that have "drawn" similarly.

*Students meet with other students who share a particular interest, placement among siblings (oldest, middle, youngest), or life experience like traveling or summer jobs.

Student Information Sheet

It can be very helpful to have current demographic information as well as educational and personal information on all of the students in your class. Depending on your needs, you may choose to solicit information about the students' background, educational preparedness, and goals. If you gather information from the students , it will probably be most beneficial if it is gathered early in the term. Students should always reserve the right to select which information they wish to share.

Some sample questions include any or all of the following.

1. What is your name? Do you have a nickname you prefer to be called in this class?

2. What is your student I.D. number?

3. Is English your native language?

4. What is your phone number and a best time to reach you?

5. What is your campus address? Home address?

6. What is your intended major?

7. What other classes are you enrolled in this term?

8. Have you attended any other colleges or universities? If yes, where have you attended?

9. Are you working? If yes, how many hours are you working?

10. Why are you attending college?

11. Are there any special challenges or concerns you have about succeeding in college?

12. How can this class be most beneficial to you? Do you have any reservations about this class?

13. What are some of your long-term goals and aspirations?

14. Who was influential to you in making the decision to come to college? Who was influential to you in selecting this particular college?

15. Do you have any physical or learning disabilities that may impact your performance in this class? Are there some ways that the instruction for this class can be accommodated or enhanced so you are able to maximize your efforts?

Please note that if a student answers affirmatively to having a physical and/or learning disability, you may be required by law to initiate a meeting with the student and make appropriate learning accommodations.

Role Playing and Case Studies

Case studies and role playing are powerful tools that bring problem-solving skills and relevance into the classroom. Both activities encourage students to put into practice the principles that they are learning in the course.

Specifically, role playing entails presenting students with a real-life or hypothetical situation that they must address by enacting how they would manage the dilemma. Role playing is rooted in the mental health and education fields, but has application to a wide variety of situations.

The Case Study method presents students with real-life problems that have generally been previously tackled by researchers, scholars, or practitioners in the field. All background information and issues critical to the case are presented to the students who must express a decision or determination about how to deal with the problem posed by the case study. Case studies have long been teaching vehicles in Law, Business, and Medicine. But most recently many other disciplines have also utilized this approach.

With both the role playing and the case study methods, there are some guiding principles to consider before beginning. First, most case studies and role playing activities work best if they appear to be viable and realistic situations. If the situation is too far fetched, the students may become disenchanted and skeptical about the value of the learning activity. Second, the role playing and case studies work best when there is some level of drama or tension in the scenario presented. A case study or role play that is too obvious or clear cut in its resolution may not engage the students' interest. Third, the case study and the role play method must engage the students in an <u>active</u> dialogue. Students must sense the complexity of the scenario presented and be prepared to express an idea or perspective even when there is a possibility that they may be incorrect in their analysis.

Most students have had minimal experience with role playing or case studies, so it is essential to introduce the students to the actual process. Students need to be prepared to engage actively in the class discussion. Unfortunately, some students view the case study method or role playing method as an opportunity to "coast" through the class. To mitigate against this attitude, students need to come to class prepared to be questioned and challenged. In addition, some students get so concerned with what they are going to say next, that they forget to *listen* to one another. Furthermore, students need to be reminded that the case study and the role playing methods are not simply an opportunity to express their personal opinion on an issue. Rather, the students' opinion should be well grounded in the concepts that have been presented in the class. At times, you as the instructor will need to remind the students about the principles and issues that should be grounding the students' questions and input.

If you utilize the role playing and case study methods, begin by gathering examples of different scenarios and materials that could be used in your class. Often individuals in a given field can offer some excellent examples of dilemmas they have encountered that would make outstanding material for a case study or role play. Observing faculty who are skilled in facilitating these approaches can also be very helpful in developing some strategies that you might include in your class.

Christensen, C.R. & Hansen, A.J.(1987). Teaching and the case study method. Boston: Harvard Business School.

Christensen, C.R., Garvin, D.A. & Sweet, A. (eds.) (1991) Education for judgement: the artistry of discussion leadership. Boston: Harvard Business School.

Ronstadt, Robert (1993). The art of case analysis. Wayland,MA.: Lord Publishing.

Accommodations for Students with Disabilities

New technology and legal mandates for accessibility have significantly increased the number of students with physical and learning disabilities within higher education. Now many capable disabled students are pursuing their own educational goals and enriching the campus environment. Virtually all institutions of higher learning are providing appropriate accommodations for students with disabilities. Some colleges and universities also provide tutoring, support groups, and special learning assistance to students with disabilities. It is essential that you as a faculty member become familiar with the policies and resources available at your particular campus. There is a wide continuum in the depth and breadth of services offered from campus to campus.

Within the classroom, you should find out what students are disabled and are requesting accommodations. An informal meeting should be established so that you and the student can discuss any special learning and testing arrangements that need to be made. Particularly, visually impaired students and some learning disabled students need to have their textbooks recorded or transferred into Braille format. In addition, library staff may need to be notified if there are any special research projects that you are assigning for the class.

Typically, the accommodations for students with disabilities are quite individualized depending on the specific disabling condition and the student's approach to learning. There are some accommodations that are frequently offered depending upon the disability. You could anticipate accommodations for certain types of disabilities to include some of the following:

Specific Learning Disabilities
> *Notetakers and/or audio-taped class sessions.
> *Extra time for exams.
> *Visual, aural, and tactile demonstrations incorporated into instruction.
> *Course and lecture outlines.
> *Computers with voice output, spelling checkers, and grammar checkers.

Mobility Impairments
> *Group assignments, notetakers/scribes, Lab assistants.
> *Extra exam time, alternative testing arrangements.
> *Classroom, labs, field trips in accessible locations.
> *Adjustable tables, lab equipment located within reach.
> *Class materials in electronic format.
> *Computers with special input devices.

Low Vision

*Large print handouts, signs, equipment labels.
*TV monitor connected to microscope to enlarge images.
*Class assignments in electronic format.
*Computer enlarged screen images.
*Seating where the light is best.

Hearing Impairments

*Interpreters, real-time captions, FM systems, note takers.
*Face student when speaking.
*Written assignments, lab instructions, demonstration summaries.
*Visual aids, visual warning system for lab emergencies.
*Repeat questions and statements from other students.
*Electronic Mail.

Blindness

*Audio-tape, Braille, or electronic lecture notes, handouts, texts.
*Describe visual aids.
*Raised-line drawing and tactile models of graphic material.
*Adaptive equipment (e.g. tactile timers, calculators, light probes)
*Computer with optical character readers, voice output, Braille screen displays, printers.
*Readers/Writers for Exams.

Health Impairments

*Notetakers, audio-taped class sessions.
*Flexible attendance requirements.
*Extra exam time, alternative testing arrangements.
*Assignments in electronic formats.
*Electronic Mail.

Diversity in the Classroom

If there is one hallmark of today's student population, it is an increasing diversity. On the other hand, faculty nationally do not reflect the same level of diversity. Therefore, it behooves all faculty members to consider how diversity and individual differences are reflected in the classroom. At this point, there is minimal research that has been conducted on how to specifically respond to ethnic, gender, and cultural diversity in the college classroom. Nevertheless, there are several principles which are likely to facilitate the establishment of a classroom ethos hospitable to all students.

To begin, there is no instructional strategy or sensitivity more important than the instructor's self-understanding of his or her own "baggage" regarding prejudice and stereotypes. To think that any American has no opinions or beliefs that reflect bias or blindspots is probably naive at best. This process of self-awareness is and should be an ongoing one. In addition, it is advisable to consider some instructional issues that will probably promote acceptance and respect within the classroom.

> Be sensitive to the text books, media, and materials that you select for the class. How are people of color depicted? Are they depicted at all? How is gender discussed? Is the language gender-free? Does the language avoid stereotyping?

> Your learning about the history and culture of various population groups makes a statement to students about your commitment to diversity. Additionally, become familiar with the leaders and scholars in your discipline who are not white and male. Many students appreciate knowing that a variety of persons have contributed to the knowledge base and practices of a given field.

> Avoid asking students of color or international students to speak on behalf of their particular ethnic, national, or cultural group. However, there may be some students of color or international students that will be eager to express their personal experience and perspective. This initiative and openness should be encouraged.

> Solicit the feedback of students regarding the climate within the classroom. Do all of the students feel respected? Are differences appreciated and validated? Are there feelings that there are variable expectations and standards for the students?

> Conduct class discussions that convey a sense of respect for all students and their viewpoints. If a student offers an offensive or racist remark during the class discussion, respond with a clear message about how the student's comment could be perceived by others. It is not advisable to ascribe motives of prejudice to the student, but rather to simply offer the feedback on the comment and its tone.

Offer a wide variety of classroom activities, assignments, and student assessment approaches which tap into individual learning strengths and cultural differences.

Encourage students to study together and to work collaboratively. The use of group activities in the class can facilitate a greater appreciation for the value of different perspectives and gifts.

Be sensitive to students that are not native English speaking individuals. It is helpful to know about the campus resources like the writing lab or an ESL program that may exist on your campus. Check in personally with students who may be experiencing some language hurdles. Many students whose first language is not English are not comfortable bringing attention to themselves during a class session.

Fleming, J.(1988) Blacks in college. San Francisco: Jossey-Bass Publishers.

Green, M.F. (ed.) (1989) Minorities on campus: a handbook for enriching diversity. Washington, D.C.: American Council on Education.

Woolbright, C. (ed.) (1989). Valuing diversity on campus: a multicultural approach. Bloomington, Ind.: Association of College Unions-International.

Written Assignments

When written assignments offer opportunities for practicing skills and problem solving relevant to the course content, then they are an important vehicle for learning. As the instructor, you have the responsibility to select written assignments that enhance the level of content mastery, creative strategies and communication competencies for your students. Your expectations for the completion of all assignments should be clearly stated and/or written and it is advisable that you actually complete any assignments yourself before giving them to students.

Students benefit most from assignments that are distributed fairly evenly throughout the term so there is not a sense of simply "cranking" out the work. Since it is becoming increasingly common that students are employed while they are attending school, they appreciate assignments that are not given out at the last minute or with only one or two days notice. Producing a "short" two- to three- page paper may not seem like much to a professor but it can wreak havoc with a student who is working an all-night shift. In addition, students can build on their competencies and you will be able to better measure the progress of your students if you give smaller, more frequent assignments. This is particularly true of first and second year college students. If you are permitting students to adapt the assignments or select an alternative topic, you need to establish some guidelines for how they should negotiate their alternative project. Students generally appreciate some variety of assignments that tap into different learning styles and needs.

In terms of your feedback and grading of the assignments, the quicker your response, the more students generally will derive from the assignment. Receiving feedback on the assignments long after subsequent assignments does not allow the opportunity for students to put into practice your observations and recommendations. Furthermore, the specific nature of your comments on the assignments facilitates a clearer understanding of what is expected on future assignments for the students. Comments like "Vague" or "Unclear" do not offer most students an adequate diagnosis of what they need to do to achieve quality work. If you are asking for specific examples or you are requesting the terminology from the class be incorporated into the written assignment, then students are clearer about what you mean by the feedback, "Vague."

In conclusion, it is important to remember the students are learning many valuable lessons about what is expected in professionally polished and academically sound work projects. It is also important to remember the students have the very difficult task of learning about the standards and expectations of more than one teacher (supervisor) every academic term.

Barrow, John C. (1986). Fostering cognitive development of students. San Francisco: Jossey-Bass Publishers.

Browne, M. Neil & Keeley, Stuart M. (1986). Asking the right questions. Englewoods, N.J.: Prentice-Hall, Inc.

Lectures That Have an Impact

The heart of the relationship between faculty and students occurs during the class session. This is the critical time when most students become engaged with the course and its content. Today, class enrollments range from 5 to 500 and classroom diversity creates challenges to faculty that are unprecedented. Educators do not need to be "entertainers" but their effectiveness will be seriously compromised if they only focus on *what* will be presented and not *how* the content will be presented.

Prior to class, it is helpful to consider thoroughly the types of activities and questions that will activate students' participation. Some faculty prepare themselves for a lecture by spending some quiet time reviewing their notes before the class. On the other hand, other faculty play upbeat music to get their adrenaline flowing. It is beneficial for you to consider what works for you in terms of intellectual and emotional preparation. In addition, it is worth your time investment to "choreograph" your class session. Have your overheads numbered, your video tape cued and your handouts ready. Take the time to predict how much time each component of your class session will take. Consider if you are trying to do too much or too little for the time allotted.

When beginning a class, students, particularly freshmen and sophomores, appreciate study tips for the class. Demonstrations of the approaches needed to read the text and how to take notes for the class are important to students who are acquiring and adapting strategies for every class. You might invite a successful student in the major to share some of his or her strategies for approaching the classes in this particular field. Or you might invite a member of your Academic Support Department to present practical tips for studying in your class.

During the class meeting time, there are a number of critical questions to consider. First, did you consider differing learning styles and cultural distinctive when planning the class? Second, is the class content clearly and succinctly presented? Are the illustrations and examples relevant and engaging? Third, is there adequate time for students to ask questions? Fourth, could students detect your enthusiasm for the course content? And finally, are the assignments and expectations explained adequately? In general, students of today appreciate when the course content is connected to the "Real World" and to the World of Work.

In summary, it is beneficial to include a post-session reflection and evaluation of each class meeting whenever your time allows. By taking a few minutes to jot down what went well, you are making an investment in your future class presentations as well as strengthening your teaching repertoire. At the same time, a few notations about what did not go smoothly facilitates future improvements for your class. Formative Assessment strategies like the "Muddiest Point" can inform your evaluation of the class session. As mentioned in the introduction, video taping or soliciting the feedback of a colleague can also provide you with valuable information for future planning and professional development.

Barrow, John C. (1986). <u>Fostering cognitive development of students</u>. San Francisco: Jossey-Bass Publishers.

Hunkins, Frances (1989) <u>Teaching thinking through effective questioning</u>. Boston:Christopher-Gordon Publishers.

Williams, Linda (1983) <u>Teaching for the two-sided mind</u>. New York: Simon and Schuster.

Teaching Older Adult Learners

Today more than half of all college students are over the age of twenty-five. A dramatic shift has occurred within college classrooms as this graying of students occurs. The median age of community college students has shifted from about 34 years of age in 1990 to a predicted 37 years of age in 2000. Older adult learners are more often than not working at least thirty hours a week and have many other major commitments besides attending college classes. Yet despite the many demands that tug on the time and energy of the older adult learner, this student is serious about education. The older adult learners usually know why they are attending college and many are experiencing significant sacrifices to make their education happen. Because of the various demands on them and their strong motivation to succeed, older adult learners are demanding of themselves and frequently are demanding of the quality of the teaching they experience.

To better serve older adult learners within the class there are some guidelines to remember as you plan and process. These guidelines are not to be construed as universally essential for all adult learners. Instead these guidelines may be helpful in creating a learning environment that is respectful and sensitive to the needs of adult learners.

1. Adult learners appreciate classes that are active and discussion focused. Most adult learners want their life experience and perspectives respected by students and faculty members.

2. Many adult learners are somewhat uncomfortable or limited in their experience on the computer and with the new trends in formatting research papers. As a faculty member, it is important that you direct older adult learners to the resources on the campus that can be of assistance in acquiring the pre-requisite skills needed for the class.

3. Do not assume that because adult learners are older than their student counterparts they are confident and assured about their abilities. Often older adult learners are somewhat insecure in the academic setting until they build up their momentum and educational track record. Prompt and specific written and verbal feedback is as important (if not more) to the older adult learner than to the traditional-aged student.

4. Remember that a number of adult learners are experiencing some physical limitations of aging like diminished eye-sight and dexterity. Be sensitive to these changes.

5. Adult learners will appreciate some options given in the assignments so they feel that they have some control over their own learning. For the adult learner, control over the learning process seems particularly important.

6. Offer examples and illustrations of course content that are taken from work and community situations and not simply from the campus. Older adult learners appreciate hearing about a circumstance that they can relate to such as parenting, professional problems, consumer issues, and community challenges, not simply examples from the residence halls using only examples of how some concept might be dealt with in the residence halls.

Brookfield, Stephen (1986). <u>Understanding and facilitating adult learning</u>. San Francisco: Jossey-Bass Publishers.

Wlodkowski, Raymond J. (1985). <u>Enhancing adult motivation to learn</u>. San Francisco: Jossey-Bass Publishers.